CLASSICS OF FREE THOUGHT

Edited by Paul Blanshard

PROMETHEUS BOOKS

Buffalo, New York

90 89 88   4 3

Library of Congress Card Catalog No. 77-73846
ISBN: 0-87975-079-0

Contents

The Capricious Cannonade

The phenomenon called the free thought movement is more like a capricious cannonade than a movement. The pattern of conduct runs something like this: Isolated iconoclasts aim their verbal weapons at the primary enemy, organized religion, and occasionally a shot reaches its mark. Then the preachers continue to preach and the doubters continue to doubt, and the world moves on.

But the effort is not wasted. Orthodoxy has been weakened and superstition reduced. The stream of culture has been slightly diverted. The world is wiser because some freethinker has dared to speak.

The capricious cannonade of free thought has been going on almost continuously during the two hundred odd years since the French Enlightenment, and it has transformed much of Western thought about religion and morals in the process. Anyone who doubts this should compare the puritanical English and American society of the late eighteenth century with the society of today. Officially both England and the United States are religious countries, England with a nominally established church and the United States with perhaps the highest average of nominal believers in God of any large modern nation.

But the credibility of the creeds is plummeting and the pulpit is losing its once-magic power. Science and philosophic realism have replaced Christian orthodoxy as the standard guides of moral behavior. In England church attendance has been reduced to a shadow, and in the United States the educated classes are increasingly skeptical about dogma, in direct proportion to their education. Try to find a high-ranking, nonseminary professor who will swallow the snake in the Garden of Eden or the whale that encompassed Jonah!

Meanwhile, our American courts have protected the unbeliever by sustaining a Jeffersonian wall of separation between church and state. Although ours is not yet a secular state—let no professed atheist try for public office!—it is rapidly becoming a true exemplar of religious freedom.

I have made no attempt in this short book to summarize the two hundred odd years of the modern free thought movement. The book is a storage house of ammunition to be used by free-thinkers in the battle against orthodoxy. I have chosen sample ammunition from thirty-six of the leading gunners of the period, and they speak for themselves. About half of my gunners have already appeared in my column of "Classics," published regularly in *The Humanist*. That magazine has been responsible for promoting this project.

For the purposes of this collection, the terms *free thought* and *classics* have been interpreted very broadly. I began my research with a historical aim, to rescue for this generation certain old gems of rationalism which had been almost forgotten. I looked backward a long way and concentrated on the very old. For working purposes I accepted the standard encyclopedic definition that a freethinker "denotes anyone who considers problems of religious history in a purely rational manner, without regard to the authority of the Church." (*Rationalism* and *freethinking* are essentially synonymous.)

Then, as I pursued this historical enterprise, I realized that classics of free thought were not limited to freethinkers, and that much documentary ammunition is recent ammunition. Some of it has been used by politicians, authors, and judges in contemporary America. If I include Tom Paine and his 1774 deist hand grenades, why should I omit H. L. Mencken, who is equally devastating? And why should I exclude Eleanor Roosevelt because she was a good Episcopalian, or John F. Kennedy because he was a strong (nominal) Roman Catholic? And should not our current Supreme Court with its very courageous stand on church-state separation receive our accolades?

So Christian Eleanor Roosevelt has been included with John Kennedy as he captured a Houston Ministers Association, and ex-priest Joseph McCabe is here with his blatant but scholarly anti-Catholicism; while Hugo Black and Felix Frankfurter have emerged as proper judicial heroes.

How should I rank these cannonaders? I started to rank them in order of their importance; but what is important? Who is the Abou Ben Adam worthy to head the battalion? I gave up and chose the alphabet. My heroes and villains have all been listed alphabetically with no distinctions.

Most of these classics are already in the open literary market. To those publishers who have kindly permitted the use of copyrighted material, I extend thanks in the appropriate places.

Paul Blanshard

St. Petersburg, Florida
January, 1977

For BEATRICE who helped a lot

Harry Elmer Barnes

Harry Elmer Barnes (1889-1968) was one of the most militant, as well as versatile, humanist scholars of this century. Starting his teaching career as a sociologist at Syracuse University, he taught social science and history at Smith, Amherst, Columbia, and the New School for Social Research. He led the attack on conventional histories of World War I, insisting that both Wilson and the Kaiser were partly responsible for the conflict. He became a famous expert on prison reform, and served for more than ten years as an editorial writer for the Scripps-Howard newspapers.

As vice president of the American Association for the Advancement of Science, he attacked religious superstition so directly that he drew the fire of Cardinal Hayes and even some of his fellow social scientists. "The chief thesis which the writer desires to advance," he said, "is that the old supernatural concepts and criteria relating to human conduct and its objectives should be discredited and abolished as rapidly as possible and supplanted by strictly secular and mundane considerations. . . . The writer is unalterably opposed to all vestiges of the old supernaturalism, with its distorted and rudimentary views of the universe, God, man, and human life."

Barnes summarized his case against superstition best in his militant 1929 book *The Twilight of Christianity*, published by the Vanguard Press. I am quoting here from his famous chapter on "The Jesus Stereotype."

—P.B.

1

The Jesus Stereotype

In circles which may in any sense be regarded as contemporaneously-minded, there is no doubt whatever that the Jesus question is by all odds the most important phase of modern religious controversy. There are three major lines of defense of the Christian religion. The first is the assumption of the inerrant and infallible nature of the Bible. The second is the dogma of the cosmic logic and complete perfection of the Christian religion. The third is the hypothesis of the uniqueness of Christ as a religious leader.

This last contention extends all the way from the Fundamentalist assumption of the virgin birth and complete deity of Jesus to the modernist contention that Jesus was a unique and perfect type of human religious teacher. The modernists have absolutely surrendered the first line of defense, and the great majority of them have abandoned the second. Yet all except a few of the advanced Unitarian Humanists and an occasional radical preacher from other denominations cling to the thesis of the uniqueness of Jesus as tenaciously as any Fundamentalist. . . . The conception of Jesus held by the general run of American modernists is as notorious an example of stereotyped thinking as any of the testimony of Mr. Bryan regarding the Bible in the course of the Dayton Trial of 1925. . . .

The Jesus issue is not merely a matter of scholarly curiosity or of interest solely to the critically-minded scholar and philosopher. It is one of the most important practical problems in the religious reconstruction of today. We can never have an intelligent and satisfactorily modernized religion until the Jesus stereotype is forever laid to rest.

As long as our religious leaders revert to the doctrine of an antique mind, which was itself insularly uninformed, as the source of their inspiration and guidance, we are bound to remain in a period of religious confusion and stagnation. Educated and critically-minded individuals, particularly among the youth of the land, can no longer be brought in great numbers to the support of an appeal which seems to them based upon foundations that challenge their historical knowledge and their sense of intellectual integrity.

As a matter of fact, the evidence for the point of view that Jesus was actually a historical character is so slight that a considerable number of the most distinguished students of New Testament times have declared Jesus to be a mythological personage, the outgrowth of the mythmaking tendencies common to religious peoples of all ages and particularly prevalent in the period of the early Roman Empire. . . . There is, in extant Jewish literature of the first century A.D., not a single authentic line making reference to Jesus. . . .

There is not in existence a single absolutely authentic passage which we may be sure literally reproduces any saying of Jesus or describes with unerring accuracy any deed or event of his life. It is particularly unfortunate that we do not have any systematic statement of his belief on any subject. Had he followed the precedent of Aristotle—assuming that he was capable of so doing—and delivered a series of lectures on history, theology, metaphysics, politics, economics, and sociology before a group of students in Jerusalem or elsewhere, we might be able to form some intelligent conception of his actual views on the leading issues of religion and society.

Far from this, we have not a single passage which we can be sure accurately reproduces Christ's views on any subject. Even accepting the Synoptic Gospels at their face value, we have only a few and often highly contradictory teachings on any important topics of religion and morality. Both pacifists and militarists are able to quote what seem to be approving passages from Jesus. Tolstoi and Gandhi could derive from Jesus the doctrine of nonresistance, while other followers of the Lamb could derive inspiration for stirring military hymns after "The Son of God Goes Forth to War." . . .

We are equally incapable of arriving at any definite picture of the personality and career of Jesus. He may have been one of the most pleasing characters in all history and he may equally well have been one of the most irritating and annoying. It would be equally foolish, on the basis of the evidence which we possess, either to eulogize or to denounce Jesus. We simply have to concede Professor Guignebert's contention that a scientific biography of Jesus is completely impossible of execution on account of the paucity of information. Alfred Loisy's picture of him as a true Jew of his times—a village workman, turned prophet, failing in his prophecy and condemned as a proletarian agitator—is probably as close to the truth as we are likely to come. . . .

In spite of the slim body of documentary material bearing upon Jesus and his teachings, and conceding that plausibility of the thesis that he was not actually a historic character, it seems to the writer more consonant with probability to conclude that Jesus was a historic personage, concerning whom we have an unfortunately small body of valuable and dependable information. . . . Even conservative scholars, thoroughly convinced of the absolute historicity of Jesus, are forced to admit that we cannot be certain, within the range of a decade at least, as to the year of Jesus' birth, and scarcely less positive regarding his death. Therefore, the selection of December 25 as the date of his birth is wholly arbitrary. He may equally well have been born on February 22, April 1 or July 4. As a matter of fact, December 25 was originally the holy day of the Mithraic occult celebrating the returning power of the sun.

Hugo Black

Hugo Lafayette Black (1886-1971) became, during his thirty-four-year stint as a Supreme Court justice, one of America's strongest defenders of religious freedom and the separation of church and state. His decisions in this area are still cited as the law and the gospel of constitutional practice.

What a strange beginning for a great judicial career! Black was the eighth child of a small-town Alabama storekeeper who died early because of drunkenness. As a boy he went to the local Primitive Baptist church, which included in its program "speaking with tongues." Later on, as a successful lawyer in Birmingham, he taught a huge Baraca Bible class in the First Baptist church. Apparently he accepted the fundamentalist and racist gospel which predominated at that time in the Southern Baptist Convention.

To succeed in Alabama politics in those days it seemed necessary for a politician to join almost everything. Black joined the Masons, Woodmen of the World, Redmen, Eagles, Elks, Knights of Pythias—and the Ku Klux Klan. One result of the joining was that he became a very popular United States senator for two terms.

When he was nominated by Roosevelt for the United States Supreme Court, a storm of protest against his old Ku Klux membership broke out in the Senate. Could a man with such a past be a good Supreme Court judge? Black survived—and answered the question in the affirmative. He grew into judicial liberalism, and he made himself one of the greatest arbiters in Supreme Court history.

I have chosen to include three excerpts from decisions which Black read in the Supreme Court; of course they were joint products. The first is his famous paragraph on the limits of religious establishment expressed in the 1947 case of *Everson* v. *Board of Education*. The second is taken from his Regent's Prayer decision in the 1962 case of *Engel* v. *Vitale*, a decision in which the Court outlawed a simple prayer in the New York public schools. The third is a sizeable extract from his decision about the rights of unbelievers in the 1961 case of *Torcaso* v. *Watkins*. This Torcaso decision destroyed many unconstitutional barnacles that had clung to local statutes, prejudicial to the rights of unbelievers. It has served as a kind of charter for the unfaithful.

The first quotation, from the 1947 Everson case, needs some explanation. Black spoke for the five to four majority of the Court in approving the use of tax funds for bus transportation for children attending Catholic parochial schools. But, having granted this comparatively modest concession to sectarian demands, he proceeded to lay down a charter of no-establishment principles in one of the strongest paragraphs in American law. Justice Frankfurter scolded him for inconsistency— quite correctly, I think—but the result was epochal. By surrendering a small outpost on the border line between church and state, the liberals won a war. Black's rules for the separation of church and state—echoing the thought of Jefferson—have become a kind of Declaration of Independence for the modern secular state.

—P.B.

The Limits of Religious Establishment

The "establishment of religion" clause of the First Amendment means at least this: Neither a state nor the federal government can set up a church. Neither can pass laws which aid one religion, aid all religions, or prefer one religion over another. Neither can force nor influence a person to go to or remain away from church against his will or force him to profess a belief or disbelief in any religion. No person can be punished for entertaining or professing religious beliefs or disbeliefs, for church attendance or nonattendance.

No tax in any amount, large or small, can be levied to support any religious activities or institutions, whatever they may be called, or whatever form they may adopt to teach or practice religion. Neither a state nor the federal government can, openly or secretly, participate in the affairs of any religious organizations or groups and vice versa. In the words of Jefferson, the clause against establishment of religion by law was intended to erect "a wall of separation between church and state."

Prayer in Public Schools

The respondent Board of Education of Union Free School District No. 9, New Hyde Park, New York, acting in its official capacity under state law, directed the school district's principal to cause the following prayer to be said aloud by each class in the presence of a teacher at the beginning of each school day:

> Almighty God, we acknowledge our dependence upon Thee, and we beg Thy blessings upon us, our parents, our teachers and our country. . . .

We think that by using its public school system to encourage recitation of the Regents' prayer, the State of New York has adopted a practice wholly inconsistent with the Establishment Clause. There can, of course, be no doubt that New York's program of daily classroom invocation of God's blessings as prescribed in the Regents' prayer is a religious activity. It is a solemn avowal of divine faith and supplication for the blessings of the Almighty. The nature of such a prayer has always been religious; none of the respondents has denied this and the trial court expressly so found. . . .

The petitioners contend among other things that the state law requiring or permitting use of the Regents' prayer must be struck down as a violation of the Establishment Clause because that prayer was composed by government officials as part of a governmental program to further religious beliefs. . . . We agree with that contention since we think that the constitutional prohibition against laws respecting an establishment of religion must at least mean that in this country it is no part of the business of government to compose official prayers for any group of the American people to recite as part of a religious program carried on by the government.

It is a matter of history that this very practice of establishing governmentally composed prayers for religious services was one of the reasons which caused many of our early colonists to leave England and seek religious freedom in American. . . .

By the time of the adoption of the Constitution, our history shows that there was a widespread awareness among many Americans of the dangers of a union of church and state. These people knew, some of them from bitter personal experience, that one of the greatest dangers to the freedom of the individual to worship in his own way lay in the government's placing its official stamp of approval upon one particular type of prayer or one particular form of religious services. . . .

The Constitution was intended to avert a part of this danger by leaving the government of this country in the hands of the people rather than in the hands of any monarch. But this safeguard was not enough. Our founders were no more willing to let the content of their prayers and their privilege of praying whenever they pleased be influenced by the ballot box than they were to let these vital matters of personal conscience depend upon the succession of monarchs. The First Amendment was added to the Constitution to stand as a guarantee that neither the power not the prestige of the federal government would be used to control, support or influence the kinds of prayer the American people can say—that the people's religion must not be subjected to the pressure of government for change each time a new political administration is elected to office. Under that amendment's prohibition against government establishment of religion, as reinforced by the provisions of the Fourteenth Amendment, government in this country, be it state or federal, is without power to prescribe by law any particular form of prayer which is to be used as an official prayer in carrying on any program of governmentally sponsored religious activity. . . . It may be appropriate to say in the words of James Madison, the author of the First Amendment: "It is proper to take alarm at the first experiment on our liberties."

The Right NOT to Believe

Article 37 of the Declaration of Rights of the Maryland Constitution provides:

> No religious test ought ever to be required as a qualification for any office of profit or trust in this State, other than a declaration of belief in the existence of God. . . .

The appellant Torcaso was appointed to the office of Notary Public by the Governor of Maryland but was refused a commission to serve because he would not declare his belief in God. He then brought this action in a Maryland Circuit Court to compel issuance of his commission, charging that the state's requirement that he declare this belief violated "the First and Fourteenth Amendments to the Constitution of the United States. . . . " The Circuit Court rejected these federal constitutional contentions, and the highest court of the state, the Court of Appeals, affirmed, holding that the state constitutional provision is self-executing and requires declaration of belief in God as a qualification for the office without need for implementing legislation. . . .

There is, and can be, no dispute about the purpose or effect of the Maryland Declaration of Rights requirement before us—it sets up a religious test which was designed to and, if valid, does bar every person who refuses to declare a belief in God from holding a public "office of profit or trust" in Maryland. The power and authority of the State of Maryland thus is put on the side of one particular sort of believers—those who are willing to say they believe in "the existence of God."

It is true that there is much historical precedent for such laws. Indeed, it was largely to escape religious test oaths and declarations that a great many of the early colonists left Europe and came here hoping to worship in their own way. It soon developed, however, that many of those who had fled to escape religious test oaths turned out to be perfectly willing, when they had the power to do so, to force dissenters from their faith to take test oaths in conformity with that faith. . . .

The effect of all this was the formal or practical "establishment" of particular religious faiths in most of the Colonies, with consequent burdens imposed on the free exercise of the faiths of nonfavored believers. . . .

We repeat and again reaffirm that neither a state nor the federal government can constitutionally force a person "to profess a belief or disbelief in any religion." Neither can constitutionally pass laws nor impose requirements which aid all religions as against non-believers, and neither can aid those religions based on a belief in the existence of God as against those religions founded on different beliefs.

(Note: Among religions in this country which do not teach what would generally be considered a belief in the existence of God are Buddhism, Taoism, Ethical Culture, Secular Humanism and others.)

This Maryland religious test for public office unconstitutionally invades the appellant's freedom of belief and religion and therefore cannot be enforced against him. The judgment of the Supreme Court of Maryland is accordingly reversed. . . .

Harry A. Blackmun

Some people believe that the most critical religious issue facing the American people today is the issue of legalized abortion. Right to Life groups, inspired and led by the Roman Catholic Church, have brought the issue into both state and presidential campaigns. Equally earnest liberal religious groups have expressed the conviction that a pregnant woman's right to an abortion is a basic constitutional right that should not be curtailed in any way.

For the time being the most important document in the struggle is the 1973 decision of the United States Supreme Court, which was expressed for the Court's majority by Justice Harry A. Blackmun. Ordinarily it would not rate as a free-thought document at all, but history has made it into such a document by force of circumstance. It expressed an important new freedom in American life, the right of a pregnant woman to choose abortion in preference to an unwanted child. And it has become important partly because America's largest and most powerful church has chosen to oppose the new right with all its political and ecclesiastical power.

Blackmun's emergence as a medical-legal scholar took the public by surprise. Could an appointee of Richard Nixon be a good judge? The public was skeptical. People did not know that this Minnesota lawyer had graduated *summa cum laude* from Harvard, and had contributed learned articles to medical journals. He had also served as counsel and director for such diverse institutions as the Mayo Clinic and a Methodist hospital. He actually knew something about medicine, and not a little about religious history.

Blackmun's emergence as a medical authority came in two cases decided on the same day, *Roe v. Wade* and *Doe v. Bolton*, in which Blackmun spoke the opinion of the majority of the Court. Jane Roe was a Texas girl, not married but pregnant, who could not secure an abortion in her own state because the right of abortion was practically limited to "saving the life of the mother." Mary Doe was a twenty-two-year-old Georgia woman, married and nine weeks pregnant who had three living children already. The two older children had been placed in a foster home because of the Doe's poverty. The youngest had been placed out for adoption. Mary Doe's husband had abandoned her for a time and she had been forced to live with her indigent parents who had eight other children to take care of. For a time Mary had become a mental patient at a state hospital, and she had no means to support the coming child. Yet Georgia law, complicated by elaborate requirements and red tape, had blocked her request for an abortion.

The Court struck down the Georgia law as unconstitutional, and in the Roe case in Texas it went far beyond these judgments, creating a new charter of free choice for pregnant women during the first two trimesters of pregnancy. The charter is so broad that it can fairly be described as abortion on demand if the demand is jointly supported by a physician and the pregnant patient. Even in the last trimester of the usual 266 days of pregnancy, the Court ruled that the power of the state to intervene is limited to serious factors.

I offer here a much abbreviated series of quotations from the historic Roe decision. The resulting church-state uproar came primarily from the Catholic bishops of the United States who, bound by the Vatican's flat rule against all abortions, assailed the Court in unprecedented fury. But it should be noted that the bishops did not speak for all American Catholics. The liberal Catholic journal *Commonweal* accepted the Court's decision as "part of the cost of living in a pluralistic and secular state," and undoubtedly millions of American Catholics concurred with this view.

More than three years after the 1973 decision Justice Blackmun, speaking again for the Court on abortion in the Danforth-Missouri case, ruled that a woman could not be denied the right of abortion simply because her husband withheld consent. Nor could an unwed teenage girl be denied abortion rights because of the lack of parental consent.

—P.B.

The Supreme Court Speaks on the Right to Choose Abortion

This Texas federal appeal and the Georgia companion . . . present constitutional challenges to state criminal abortion legislation. The Texas statutes under attack here are typical of those that have been in effect in many states for approximately a century. . . .

We forthwith acknowledge our awareness of the sensitive and emotional nature of the abortion controversy, of the vigorous opposing views, even among physicians, and of the deep and seemingly absolute convictions that the subject inspires. One's philosophy, one's experiences, one's attitude toward the family and their values, and the moral standards one establishes and seeks to observe, are all likely to influence and to color one's thinking and conclusions about abortion.

In addition, population growth, pollution, poverty, and racial overtones tend to complicate and not to simplify the problem.

Our task, of course, is to resolve the issue by constitutional measurement free of emotion and of predilection. We seek earnestly to do this, and because we do, we have inquired into, and in this opinion place some emphasis upon medical and medical-legal history and what the history reveals about man's attitudes toward the abortive procedure over the centuries. . . .

Jane Roe, a single woman who was residing in Dallas County, Texas, instituted this federal action in March 1970 against the district attorney of the county. She sought a declaratory judgment that the Texas criminal abortion statutes were unconstitutional on their face, and an injunction restraining the defendant from enforcing the statutes.

Roe alleges that she was unmarried and pregnant; that she

wished to terminate her pregnancy by an abortion "performed by a competent, licensed physician, under safe, clinical conditions"; that she was unable to get a "legal" abortion in Texas because her life did not appear to be threatened by the continuation of her pregnancy; and that she could not afford to travel to another jurisdiction in order to secure a legal abortion under safe conditions. She claimed that the Texas statutes were unconstitutionally vague and that they abridged her right of personal privacy, protected by the First, Fourth, Fifth, Ninth, and Fourteenth Amendments. . . .

It is perhaps not generally appreciated that the restrictive criminal abortion laws in effect in a majority of states today are of relatively recent vintage. These laws, generally proscribing abortion or its attempt at any time during pregnancy except when necessary to preserve the pregnant woman's life, are not of ancient or even of common-law origin. Instead, they derive from statutory changes effected, for the most part, in the latter half of the nineteenth century. . . . Greek and Roman law afforded little protection to the unborn. If abortion was prosecuted in some places, it seems to have been based on a concept of a violation of the father's right to his offspring. Ancient religion did not bar abortion. . . . Most Greek thinkers . . . commended abortion, at least prior to viability. . . .

It is undisputed that at the common law, abortion performed *before* "quickening"—the first recognizable movement of the fetus *in utero,* appearing usually from the sixteenth to the eighteenth week of pregnancy—was not an indictable offense. . . . Although Christian theology and the canon law came to fix the point of animation at forty days for a male and eighty days for a female, a view that persisted until the nineteenth century, there was otherwise little agreement about the precise time of formation or animation. There was agreement, however, that prior to this point the fetus was to be regarded as part of the mother and its destruction, therefore, was not homicide. . . .

It is thus apparent that at common law, at the time of the adoption of our Constitution, and throughout the major portion of the nineteenth century, abortion was viewed with less disfavor than under most American statutes currently in effect. Phrasing it another way, a woman enjoyed a substantially broader right to terminate a pregnancy than she does in most states today. . . .

When most criminal abortion laws were first enacted, the procedure was a hazardous one for the woman. This was particularly true prior to the development of antisepsis. . . . Modern medical techniques have altered this situation. . . . Abortion in early pregnancy, that is, prior to the end of first trimester, although not without its risks, is now relatively safe. Mortality rates for women undergoing early abortions, where the procedure is legal, appear to be as low as or lower than the rates for normal childbirth. . . .

The Constitution does not specifically mention any right of privacy. In a line of decisions, however, . . . the Court has recognized that a right of personal privacy, or a guarantee of certain areas or zones of privacy, does exist under the Constitution. . . . This right of privacy . . . is broad enough to encompass a woman's decision whether or not to terminate her pregnancy. The detriment that the state would impose upon the pregnant woman by denying this choice altogether is apparent. Specific and direct harm medically diagnosable even in early pregnancy may be involved. Maternity, or additional offspring, may force upon the woman a distressful life and future. Psychological harm may be imminent. Mental and physical health may be taxed by child care. There is also the distress for all concerned, associated with the unwanted child, and there is the problem of bringing a child into a family already unable, psychologically and otherwise, to care for it. In other cases as in this one, the additional difficulties and continuing stigma of unwed motherhood may be involved. All these are factors the woman and her responsible physician necessarily will consider in consultation. . . . We therefore conclude that the right of personal privacy includes the abortion decision, but that this right is not unqualified and must be considered against important state interests in regulation. . . .

The appellee and certain *amici* argue that the fetus is a "person" within the language and meaning of the Fourteenth Amendment. In support of this they outline at length and in detail the well-known facts of fetal development. If this suggestion of personhood is established, the appellent's case, of course, collapses, for the fetus's right to life is then guaranteed specifically by the

Amendment. . . . The appellee conceded on reargument that no case could be cited that holds that a fetus is a person within the meaning of the Fourteenth Amendment. . . . All this, together with our observation . . . that throughout the major portion of the nineteenth century prevailing legal abortion practices were far freer than they are today, persuades us that the word "person," as used in the Fourteenth Amendment, does not include the unborn. . . .

There has always been strong support for the view that life does not begin until live birth. This was the view of the Stoics. It appears to be the predominant, though not the unanimous, attitude of the Jewish faith. It may be taken to represent also the position of a large segment of the Protestant community, insofar as that can be ascertained. . . . In short, the unborn have never been recognized in the law as persons in the whole sense. In view of all this, we do not agree that by adopting one theory of life, Texas may override the rights of the pregnant woman that are at stake. . . .

To summarize . . .

(a) For the stage prior to approximately the end of the first trimester, the abortion decision and its effectuation must be left to the medical judgment of the pregnant woman's attending physician.

(b) For the stage subsequent to approximately the end of the first trimester, the state in promoting its interest in the health of the mother, may, if it chooses, regulate the abortion procedure in ways that are reasonably related to maternal health.

(c) For the stage subsequent to viability the state, in promoting its interest in the potentiality of human life, may, if it chooses, regulate, and even proscribe abortion except where it is necessary, in appropriate medical judgment, for the preservation of the life or health of the mother. . . .

This holding, we feel, is consistent with the relative weights of the respective interests involved, with the lessons and example of medical and legal history, with the lenity of the common law, and with the demands of the profound problems of the present day. . . .

Charles Bradlaugh

Charles Bradlaugh (1833-1891), the famous English freethinker, has often been compared with Robert Ingersoll because the two were contemporaries and they talked about the same things, chiefly the Bible and the shortcomings of Christian orthodoxy. But Bradlaugh was distinctly proletarian while Ingersoll was not. Ingersoll was elegant in his eloquence; Bradlaugh was effectively crude. Both men achieved great success as lecturers, and both were partially defeated in their political aspirations by their notorious unbelief.

Bradlaugh was born in London as the oldest of seven children of a nurse maid and a solicitor's clerk. He quit school at the age of eleven to work as an errand boy at ten shillings a week. He discovered that he liked to talk in public. He began his talking career as a Sunday school teacher in the Church of England but was soon dropped when his teaching promoted "atheistical questions" among his pupils. He decided when he was twenty that he was an unbeliever, and by the time he was twenty-six he had already outtalked a clergyman in a public debate.

Running for Parliament, he was at first badly defeated, but later, in 1881, he scored a popular success at the polls. But then he was denied his seat in the House of Commons because of the English law requiring members of the House to take an oath affirming dependence on the Deity.

Bradlaugh, of course, refused to conform and launched his six-year campaign against the law. He was not accepted as a member of Parliament until in 1882 when he marched down the House floor to the Speaker, produced a Bible from his pocket and administered the oath to himself without any Deity in it. As Sir Leslie Stephen pointed out in a brilliant defense of Bradlaugh (*Fortnightly Review*, Vol. 39, 1880) "[I]f all the secularists and atheists in the kingdom had asked how to advance their opinions, they could not have devised a better scheme than the Bradlaugh agitation."

Bradlaugh was equally successful in his campaign against government censorship of his small, free-thought journal, *The National Reformer*. Required to give sureties against blasphemous libel, he long carried an inscription on the front page: "Printed in Defiance of Her Majesty's Government." He fought successfully against the English law that required witnesses to believe in a future state of reward or punishment.

His defiance included the whole range of Christian dogma. "The so-called belief in Creation," he said, "is nothing more than the prostitution of the intellect on the threshold of the unknown. . . . Religious belief is powerful in proportion to the want of scientific knowledge on the part of the believer. The more ignorant the more credulous." But in 1889 he failed to persuade the House of Commons to repeal the antiblasphemy laws.

That Bradlaugh was not a great scholar was apparent in his definitions of atheism. He defined the term as equivalent to agnosticism. In 1862 he declared: "Denial of God is Netheism. An atheist says, 'I am ignorant; I do not know what you mean by the word; I am without any idea of God; to me the word *God* is a word conveying no meaning. The Bible God I deny; the Christian God I disbelieve in; but I am not rash enough to say there is no God as long as you tell me you are unprepared to define God to me.'"

Bradlaugh was more than an atheist. He was a very courageous social reformer. As a convinced Republican he opposed the English monarchy and favored Irish independence. He also supported the incipient birth control movement. With his then-associate, Annie Besant, he was convicted of circulating one of England's first birth control pamphlets. These two rebels escaped imprisonment only because of a technical flaw in their indictment.

The following typical selection is taken from Bradlaugh's *About the Devil and Other Essays*, published by Charles Somerby in 1875.

—P.B.

God, Adam, and Atonement

Adam's sin is the cornerstone of Christianity, the keystone of the arch. Without the fall there is no redeemer, for there is no fallen one to be redeemed. . . .

Did Adam sin? We will take the Christian's Bible in our hands to answer the question. . . . The Bible story is that a deity created one man and one woman; that he placed them in a garden wherein he had also placed a tree which was good for food, pleasant to the eyes, and a tree to be desired to make one wise. . . . He commanded them not to eat of the fruit of this attractive tree, under penalty of death. . . .

If the All-wise had intended the tree to be avoided, would he have made its allurements as overpowering to the senses? . . . The tempter is stronger than the tempted; the witchery of the serpent is too great for the spellbound woman; the decoy tree is too potent in its temptations; overpersuaded herself by the honey-tongued voice of the seducer, she plucks the fruit and gives to her husband also. And for this their offspring are to suffer!

The yet unborn are to be the victims of God's vengeance on their parents' weakness—though he had made them weak. . . . It is for this fall that Jesus is to atone. He is sacrificed to redeem the world's inhabitants from the penalties for a weakness they had no share in.

It was not sin, for the man was influenced by circumstances prearranged by the Deity, and which man was powerless to resist or control. But if man was so influenced by such circumstances, then it was God who influenced man, God who punished the human race for an action to the commission of which he impelled their progenitor.

Adam did not sin. He ate the fruit of a tree which God had made good to be eaten. He was induced to this through the indirect persuasion of a serpent God had made purposely to persuade him. . . . What have we to do with their sin? We, unborn when the act was committed and without choice as to coming into the world? . . .

If the atonement is for the whole world, does it extend to unbelievers as well as believers in the efficacy? If it only includes believers, then what has become of those generations who, according to the Bible, for 4,000 years succeeded each other in the world without faith in Christ because without knowledge of his mission? Should not Jesus have come 4,000 years earlier, or, at least, should he not have come when the ark on Ararat served as a monument of God's merciless vengeance, which had made the whole earth a battlefield whereon the omnipotent had crushed the feeble, and had marked his prowess by the innumerable myriads of decayed dead? . . .

Japanese, Chinese, savage Indians, Kaffirs, and others have surely a right to complain of this atonement scheme which insures them eternal damnation by making it requisite to believe in a Gospel of which they have no knowledge. . . . Then what becomes of a child that only lives a few hours, is never baptized, and, never having any mind, consequently never has any belief? What becomes of one idiot born who, throughout his dread life, never has mental capacity for the acceptance or examination of any religious dogmas whatever? Is the idiot saved who cannot believe? I, with some mental faculties tolerably developed, cannot believe. Must I be damned? If so, fortunate short-lived baby! Lucky idiot!

That the atonement should not be effective until the person to be saved has been baptized is at least worthy of comment; that the sprinkling of a few drops of water should quench the flames of hell is a remarkable feature in the Christian's creed. . . .

How many fiery quarrels have raged on the formula of baptism among those loving brothers in Christ who believe he died for them! How strange an idea that, though God has been crucified to redeem mankind, it yet needs the font of water to wash away the lingering stain of man's crime!

Luther Burbank

For a few weeks in 1926 the most noted "infidel" in the world was the famous California plant wizard, Luther Burbank. A reporter friend from the *Oakland Post-Inquirer* had asked him what he thought about Henry Ford's ideas of immortality. He replied: "I am an infidel. . . . Jesus Christ was an infidel." The storm that broke around his head was a national sensation. Six ministers in his hometown of Santa Rosa, California, publicly condemned him. The *WCTU* held a prayer meeting for his soul.

Luther Burbank (1849-1926) was one of those self-educated geniuses who came to an essentially humanist position in religion without the benefit of philosophy or formal theological training. The thirteenth child of a Massachusetts farmer and pottery-manufacturer, he had read a bit of Charles Darwin and had studied medicine informally for a few months; but his formal education stopped at the high-school level. He started life as a market gardener, and soon demonstrated that he had a magic thumb by producing "the Burbank potato." Moving to California, he established himself as probably the most famous experimenter in plant science in all history. His magic touch extended to fruit, flowers, and vegetables.

He was naively astonished by the storm over his "infidelity" and decided to set himself right with the public by accepting the invitation of the First Congregational Church of San Francisco to preach a sermon about his own faith. It was an innocent sermon, full of love and honesty. His thin voice—he was nearly seventy-seven, with streaming white hair— barely reached the huge overflow congregation. He died shortly afterward, and Judge Ben B. Lindsey of Denver, in an address at his grave, declared: "Though his spirit was as sweet as the gentlest zephyr that ever kissed his favorite roses, it did not save him from the bigotry of an age still idolatrous, still savage in its intolerance."

I reprint herewith part of that sermon. The entire text is to be found in an excellent book, *Luther Burbank: The Wizard and the Man,* by Ken and Pat Kraft (New York: Meredith Press, 1967).

—P.B.

Our Savior, Science

I love everybody! I love everything! . . . I love humanity, which has been a constant delight to me during all my seventy-seven years of life; and I love flowers, trees, animals, and all the works of Nature as they pass before us in time and space. What a joy life is when you have made a close working partnership with Nature, helping her to produce for the benefit of mankind new forms, new colors, and perfumes in flowers which were never known before. . . .

All things—plants, animals, and men—are already in eternity traveling across the face of time, whence we know not, whither who is able to say. Let us have one world at a time and let us make the journey one of joy to our fellow passengers. . . .

I love to look into the fearless, honest, trusting eyes of a child, who so long has been said by theologians to be conceived and born in sin and pre-damned at birth. Do you believe all our teachers without question? I cannot. . . .

If my words have awakened thought in narrow bigots and petrified hypocrites, they will have done their appointed work. The universal voice of science tells us that the consequences fall upon ourselves here and now, if we misuse this wonderful body, or mind, or the all-prevading spirit of good. Why not accept these plain facts and guide our lives accordingly? We must not be deceived by blind leaders of the blind, calmly expecting to be "saved" by anyone except by the Kingdom within ourselves. The truly honest and brave ones know that if they are to be saved it must be by their own efforts. . . .

The religion of most people is what they would like to believe, not what they do believe, and very few people stop to examine its foundation underneath. The idea that a good God would send people to a burning hell is utterly damnable to me—the ravings of insanity, superstition gone to seed!

I don't want to have anything to do with such a God. I am a lover of man and of Christ as a man and his work, and all things that help humanity; but nevertheless, just as he was an infidel then, I am an infidel today. I prefer and claim the right to worship the infinite, everlasting, almighty God of this vast universe as revealed to us gradually, step by step, by the demonstrable truths of our savior, science.

J. B. Bury

John Bagnell Bury (1861-1927) was born in Ireland, educated at Trinity College, Dublin, and died in Rome. But he belonged to England. His best twenty-five years were spent as Regius Professor of Modern History at Cambridge. Although he was a scholar's scholar, producing vast and learned works about the Roman Empire, his peculiar gift was the ability to write about free thought and orthodoxy in language that the common man could understand. In this respect he was paralleled by another writer he admired but who lived in an entirely different world. I refer to Tom Paine. Bury did much to redeem Paine's damaged reputation.

Bury's bias—perhaps it should be called optimism—was a bias in favor of the rational mind, which he fondly believed would some day triumph over all obstacles. One of his books was called *The Idea of Progress,* and he made it clear he believed the world was curable.

From the American point of view Bury's most important work was *A History of Freedom of Thought.* In it he marshalled in readable style the basic facts about man's battle against organized religious superstition. His hero was the completely rational man devoted to the principles of science. Although he could never be described as a social revolutionist, he was one of the most influential English scholars to emphasize the relationship of class exploitation to religious ignorance. In describing the suppression of unorthodox opinion he said: "The unconfessed motive has been fear of the people. Theology has been regarded as a good instrument for keeping the poor in order, and unbelief as a cause or accompaniment of dangerous political opinions."

At least one important book by Bury was published after his death, his *History of the Papacy in the Nineteenth Century.* It is a vivid story of papal political manipulation. It contains Bury's exposé of Pius IX's 1864 Syllabus of Errors.

I have chosen excerpts from *A History of Free Thought* concerned with the rise and persecution of Tom Paine. The work was published by Henry Holt in 1913.

—P.B.

The Battles of Tom Paine

The list of the English deistic writers of the eighteenth century closes with one whose name is more familiar than any of his predecessors, Thomas Paine. A Norfolk man, he migrated to America and played a leading part in the Revolution. Then he returned to England and in 1791 published his *Rights of Man* in two parts. . . .

At this time it was as dangerous to publish revolutionary opinions in politics as in theology. Paine was an enthusiastic admirer of the American Constitution and a supporter of the French Revolution (in which also he was to play a part). His *Rights of Man* is an indictment of the monarchical form of government, and a plea for representative democracy. It had an enormous sale, a cheap edition was issued, and the government finding that it was accessible to the poorer classes, decided to prosecute. . . . Paine was found guilty and outlawed.

He soon committed a new offense by the publication of an anti-Christian work, *The Age of Reason* (1794 and 1796), which he began to write in the Paris prison into which he had been thrown by Robespierre. This book is remarkable as the first important English publication in which the Christian scheme of salvation and the Bible are assailed in plain English without any disguise or reserve. In the second place, it was written in such a way as to reach the masses. And, thirdly, while the criticisms of the Bible are in the same vein as those of the earlier deists, Paine is the first to present with force the incongruity of the scheme with the conception of the universe attained by astronomical science.

(He said) "Though it is not a direct article of the Christian system that this world that we inhabit is the whole of the inhabitable globe, yet it is so worked up therewith—from what is called the mosaic account of the creation, the story of Eve and the apple, and the counterpart of that story, the death of the Son of God—that to believe otherwise (that is, to believe that God created a plurality of worlds at least as numerous as what we call stars) renders the Christian system of faith at once little and ridiculous, and scatters it in the mind like feathers in the air. The two beliefs cannot be held together in the same mind; and he who thinks he believes both has thought but little of either." ...

It was doubtless in consequence of the enormous circulation of *The Age of Reason* that a Society for the Suppression of Vice decided to prosecute the publisher. Unbelief was common among the ruling class, but the view was firmly held that religion was necessary for the populace and that any attempt to disseminate unbelief among the lower classes must be suppressed. Religion was regarded as a valuable instrument to keep the poor in order. ...

At the trial (1797) the judge placed every obstacle in the way of the defense. The publisher was sentenced to a year's imprisonment. This was not the end of Paine prosecutions. In 1811 a third part of *The Age of Reason* appeared, and Eaton, the publisher, was condemned to eighteen months' imprisonment and to stand in the pillory once a month. The judge, Lord Ellenborough, said in his charge that "to deny the truths of the book which is the foundation of our faith has never been permitted."

The poet Shelley addressed to Lord Ellenborough a scathing letter. "Do you think to convert Mr. Eaton to your religion by embittering his existence? You might force him by torture to profess your tenets, but he could not believe them except you should make them credible, which perhaps exceeds your power. Do you think to please the God you worship by this exhibition of your zeal? If so, the demon to whom some nations offer human hectacombs is less barbarous than the deity of civilized society!"

In 1819 Richard Carlyele was prosecuted for publishing *The Age of Reason* and sentenced to a large fine and three years' imprisonment. Unable to pay the fine, he was kept in prison for three years. His wife and sister, who carried on the business and continued to sell the book, were fined and imprisoned soon afterwards with a whole host of shop assistants.

If his publishers suffered in England, the author himself suffered in America, where bigotry did all it could to make the last years of his life bitter.

Morris R. Cohen

Morris Raphael Cohen (1880-1947) attained his greatest fame as a teacher and philosopher at the College of the City of New York, where he taught for twenty-six years.

Born in Minsk and coming to America at the age of twelve, he took his Ph.D. at Harvard in 1906 and went directly to City College where he soon became a popular institution. He served for a time as president of the American Philosophical Association and authored many important books in the field of philosophy.

He soon became known, in spite of his mild manners, as a determined foe of the superstitions of organized religion, both Christianity and Judaism. He was an intellectual socialist who tried to yield his post for a time to Bertrand Russell in the famous battle from which Russell was excluded. (See Russell.)

Such a learned and mild-mannered gentleman was a perfect critic of religion to serve as the devil's advocate in religious controversy. Perhaps that is one reason why Cohen accepted the challenge to serve as such an advocate in a formal debate. He called his piece "The Dark Side of Religion," and he poured into his contribution all the caustic criticism of organized religious life that he could think of. But he was careful to point out that he was not producing such a negative epic for the sake of controversy. He really believed his negative arraignment, and he said so. He considered religion—most religion—intolerably alien to intelligence. He concluded his bitter indictment by saying: "I do not wish to suggest that I am merely an advocate, or that I have any doubts as to the justice of the arguments that I have advanced. . . . I hold them all in good faith."

Cohen's entire piece was printed unabridged in his *The Faith of a Liberal,* published by Henry Holt and Company, which has kindly given permission to reprint. I have used fragments.

—P.B.

The Dark Side of Religion

The *advocatus diaboli*, as you know, is not a lawyer employed by the Prince of Darkness. He is a faithful member of the Church whose duty it is, when it is proposed to canonize a saint, to search out all the opposing considerations and to state them as cogently as possible. This wise institution compels the advocates of canonization to exert themselves to develop arguments vigorous enough to overcome all objections. In this symposium on religion, I am asked to serve as *advocatus diaboli;* to state the dark side so that those who follow may have definite positions to attack and may thus more fully develop the strength of their case.

While there have not been wanting atheists and other free-thinkers who have attacked religion root and branch, these assailants have often shared the indiscriminate or fanatical intensity which has characterized so many upholders of religion. It has therefore been possible to pass over the argument of men like Voltaire, Bradlaugh, or Ingersoll, as inaccurate, superficial, and too one-sided. The truth, however, is that religion is something about which men generally are passionate; and it is as difficult to be patient with those who paint its defects as it is to listen attentively to those who point out our most intimate failings or the shortcoming of those we love most dearly, of our family, or of our country. . . .

But such tacit beliefs do become at times explicit, and when this happens, men cling to the verbal formula with the most amazing intensity and tenacity. Men are willing to burn others and to be burned themselves on the question whether they should cross themselves with one finger or two, or whether God is one person of various aspects or natures, or three persons of one substance.

Since the days of the Greek philosopher Xenophanes, theistic religion has been accused of foolish anthropomorphism. And since Epicurus and Lucretius it has been identified by many thinkers with superstition. Eighteenth- and nineteenth-century writers like Voltaire, Gibbon, and Condorcet, Lecky, Draper, and A. D. White have so traced the history of the conflict between scientific enlightenment and religious obscurantism as to make this point a commonplace. But the attempt has been made to make it appear that this conflict is not between religion and science, but between the latter and theology. This seems to me a cheap and worthless evasion.

In the first place, none of the religions that are in the field today ever have dispensed or can dispense with all theology. What would be left today of Christianity, Judaism, or Islam without a belief in a personal God to whom we can pray? In the second place, we do not understand the roots of religion if we do not see that the historic opposition to science has not been a vagary of wicked theologians but has risen out of the very spirit that has animated most, if not all, of the religions that have appeared in history. We must start with the fact that with rare exceptions men cling to the religion in which they are born and to which they have been habituated from childhood. We inherit our traditional ritual with its implicit faith and emotional content almost with our mother's milk; and we naturally cling to it as passionately as we do to all things that have thus become part of our being, our family, our country, or our language. . . .

To religion, agreement is a practical and emotional necessity, and doubt is a challenge and an offense. We cannot tolerate those who wish to interfere or break up the hallowed customs of our group. Science, on the other hand, is a game in which opposing claims only add zest and opportunity. If the foundation of Euclidean geometry or Newtonian physics are suddenly questioned, some individual scientists may show their human limitations; but science as a whole has its field widened thereby, great enthusiasm is created for new investigations, and the innovators are objects of grateful general homage. Science does not need, therefore, to organize crusades to kill off heretics or unbelievers. Science, like art, enjoys its own activity and this enjoyment is not interfered with by anyone who obstinately refuses to join the game or scoffs at what the scientist has proved. The scientific banquet is not spoiled by our neighbors' refusing to enjoy it.

Thus it comes to pass that religion passionately clings to traditional beliefs which science may overthrow to satisfy its insatiable curiosity and its desire for logical consistency. The conflict between religion and science is thus a conflict between (on the one hand) loyalty to the old and (on the other) morally neutral curiosity about everything. . . .

The fetish-worshiper attaches magical potency to stones, but so does the Bible. Touching the Ark, even with the most worshipful intention, brings death. Christianity frowns on idol-worshiping but it still attaches supernatural power to certain objects like the cross, relics of saints, and so on. Holy water wards off devils. Miracles are a part of Christian faith and are offered as evidence of its truth. But the evidence in favor of the Virgin Birth, of the stopping of the sun and the moon at Ajalon, or of the Resurrection, cannot support its own weight. A small part of mankind finds it adequate, and this only because of the fear of being damned or anathematized for unbelief. It is inconceivable that an impartial court would convict anybody on such evidence. . . .

It is not necessary for me to recount the fight of Christianity against the Copernican astronomy, against modern geology or biology, or against the scientific treatment of biblical history. They have become commonplace, and I may merely refer to the works of Lecky, Draper, A.D. White, and Benn. The point to be noted is that the old adherents of religion did not want to know the truth, and that their religion did not encourage them to think it worth while to seek any truth other than their accepted particular faith. Religious truth is absolute and its possession makes everything else unimportant. . . .

In this respect "liberal" modernism seems intellectually much more corrupting than orthodox Fundamentalism. Confronted by natural absurdities—such as the sun and the moon stopping in their course, or the hare chewing the cud—the Fundamentalist can still say: "I believe in the word of the Spirit more than in the evidence offered by the eyes of my corruptible flesh." This recog-

nizes a clear conflict; and the intellectual hara-kiri of the Fundamentalist is a desperate venture that can appeal only to those
whose faith is already beyond human reason or evidence. But the
modernist who gives up the infallibility of the Bible in matters of
physics, and tries to keep it in matters of faith and morals, has to
resort to intellectually more corrupting procedure. By "liberal"
and unhistorical interpretations he tries—contrary to the maxim
of Jesus—to pour new wine into old bottles and then pretend that
the result *is* the ancient wine of moral wisdom.

In the struggle for social justice, what has been the actual influence of religion? Here the grandiose claims of religious
apologists are sadly belied by historic facts. The frequent claim
that Christianity abolished slavery has nothing but pious wishes
to support it. Indeed, in our own country, the clergy of the South
was vigorously eloquent in defense of slavery as a divine institution. Nor was it the Church that was responsible for the initiation
of the factory legislation that mitigated the atrocious exploitation
of human beings in mines and mills. It was not the Church that
initiated the movement to organize workmen for mutual support
and defense, or that originated the effort to abolish factual slavery
when men were paid in orders on company stores—a practice that
has prevailed in some of our own states. The Church has generally
been on the side of the powerful classes who have supported it—
royalists in France, landowners in England, the *cientifico* or ex-
ploiting class in Mexico. Here and there some religious leader
or group has shown sympathy with the oppressed; but the Church
as a whole has property interests that affiliate it with those in
power. . . .

I have spoken of the dark side of religion and have thus
implied that there is another side. But if this implication puts me
out of the class of those who are unqualified opponents of all that
has been called religion, I do not wish to suggest that I am merely
an advocate, or that I have any doubts as to the justice of the arguments that I have advanced. Doubtless some of my arguments
may turn out to be erroneous, but at present I hold them all in
good faith.

Clarence Darrow

Clarence Seward Darrow (1857-1938) has practically become a labor-liberal saint in recent years, due in part to Henry Fonda's magnificent portrayal of him on the stage. Although his fame was based primarily upon his courtroom performances in several great labor cases, Darrow was almost equally famous for his firm stand against religious superstition. He frequently referred to his own religious doubts even when addressing conventional jurors. He coupled his agnosticism with a despairing kindness. "The best that we can do," he said in his autobiography, "is to be kindly and helpful toward our friends and fellow passengers who are clinging to the same speck of dirt while we are drifting side by side to our common doom."

The climax of Darrow's career came in July 1925 when he examined William Jennings Bryan in the Scopes trial before three thousand sweating spectators in Dayton, Tennessee. Unfortunately the Darrow-Bryan exchange is too wandering and discursive for this book; readers who are interested in the text may find the most important parts in Arthur Weinberg's *Attorney For the Damned.*

Darrow was a very talkative man, most effective when he had no manuscript before him. He talked to the jury eleven hours to win freedom for Big Bill Haywood when Haywood was charged with the murder of former Governor Stunenberg of Idaho in 1907.

I knew Darrow slightly. His chief assistant in the Scopes trial was my old law-office boss, Arthur Garfield Hays. The religious convictions of Darrow, Hays, and myself were approximately equal—that is, approximately zero. I have selected a little-known but wholly typical sample of Darrow at his talking best, an obviously adlib speech published without date and without copyright in Little Blue Book No. 1637.

—P.B.

33

Absurdities of the Bible

Why am I agnostic? Because I don't believe some of the things that other people say they believe. Where do you get your religion, anyway? I won't bother to discuss just what religion is, but I think a fair definition of religion could take account of two things, at least, immortality and God, and that both of them are based on some book, so practically all of it is a book.

As I have neither the time not the learning to discuss every religious book on earth, and as I live in Chicago, I am interested in the Christian religion. So I will discuss the book that deals with the Christian religion. Is the Bible the work of anything but man? Of course, there is no such book as the Bible. The Bible is made up of sixty-six books, some of them written by various authors at various times, covering a period of about one thousand years— all the literature that they could find over a period longer than the time that has elapsed since the discovery of America down to the present time.

Is the Bible anything but a human book? Of course those who are believers take both sides of it. If there is anything that troubles them, "We don't believe this." Anything that doesn't trouble them they do believe.

What about its accounts of the origin of the world? What about its account of the first man and the first woman? Adam was the first, made about less than six thousand years ago. Well, of course, every scientist knows that human beings have been on the earth at least a half-million years, probably more. Adam got lonesome and they made a companion for him. That was a good day's work—or a day's work, anyhow.

FROM RIB TO WOMAN

They took a simple way to take one of Adam's ribs and cut it out and make it into a woman.

Now, is that story a fact or a myth? How many preachers would say it was a myth? None! There are some people who still occupy Christian pulpits who say it is, but they used to send them to the stake for that.

If it isn't true, then what is? How much did they know about science in those days, how much did they know about the heavens and the earth? The earth was flat, or did God write that down, or did the old Hebrew write it down because he didn't know any better and nobody else then knew any better?

What was the heavens? The sun was made to light the day and the moon to light the night. The sun was pulled out in the day time and taken in at night and the moon was pulled across after the sun was taken out. I don't know what they did in the dark of the moon. They must have done something.

The stars, all there is about the stars, "the stars he made also." They were just "also."

Did the person who wrote that know anything whatever about astronomy? Not a thing. They believed they were just little things up in the heavens, in the firmament, just a little way above the earth, about the size of a diamond in an alderman's shirt stud. They always believed it until astronomers came along and told them something different.

Adam and Eve were put in a garden where everything was lovely and there were no weeds to hoe down. They were allowed to stay there on one condition, and that is that they didn't eat of the tree of knowledge. That has been the condition of the Christian church from then until now. They haven't eaten as yet, as a rule they do not.

They were expelled from the garden, Eve was tempted by the snake who presumably spoke to her in Hebrew. And she fell for it and of course Adam fell for it, and then they were driven out. How many believe that story today?

If the Christian church doesn't believe it why doesn't it say so? You do not find them saying that. If they do not believe it here and there, someone says it. That is, he says it at great danger to his immortal soul, to say nothing of his good standing in his church.

The snake was cursed to go on his belly after that. How he went before, the story doesn't say. And Adam was cursed to work. That is why we have to work. That is, some of us—not I.

And Eve and all of her daughters to the end of time were condemned to bring forth children in pain and agony. Lovely God, isn't it? Lovely!

CAN'T BELIEVE STORY

If that story was necessary to keep me out of hell and put me in heaven—necessary for my life—I wouldn't believe it because I couldn't believe it.

I do not think any God could have done it and I wouldn't worship a God who would. It is contrary to every sense of justice that we know anything about.

God had a great deal of trouble with the earth after he made it. People were building a tower—the Tower of Babel—so that they could go up and peek over.

God didn't want them to do that and so he confounded their tongues. A man would call up for a pail of mortar and they would send him up a tub of suds, or something like that. They couldn't understand each other.

Is that story true? How did they happen to write it? They found there were various languages, and that is the origin of the languages. Everybody knows better today.

Is that story true? Did God write it? H must have known; he must have been all-knowing then as he is all-knowing now.

I do not need to mention them. You remember that joyride that Balaam was taking on the ass. That was the only means of locomotion they had besides walking. It is the only one pretty near what they have now. Balaam wanted to get along too fast and he was beating the ass and the ass turned around and asked him what he was doing it for. In Hebrew, of course. It must have been in Hebrew for Balaam was a Jew.

AND JOSHUA SAID TO THE SUN, "STAND STILL."

Is that true or is it a story?

And Joshua; you remember about Joshua. He was a great general. Very righteous and he was killing a lot of people and he hadn't quite finished the job and so he turned to the mountain top and said to the sun, "Stand still till I finish this job," and it stood still.

Is that one of the true ones or one of the foolish ones?

There are several things that that does. It shows how little they knew about the earth and day and night. Of course, they thought that if the sun stood still it wouldn't be pulled along any further and the night wouldn't come on. We know that if it had stood still from that day to this it wouldn't have affected the day or night; that is affected by the revolution of the earth on its axis.

Is it true? Am I wicked because I know it cannot possibly be true? Have you got to get rid of all your knowledge and all your common sense to save your soul?

Wait until I am a little older; maybe I can then. But my friend says that he doesn't believe those stories. They are figurative.

Are they figurative? Then what about the New Testament? Why does he believe these stories?

Here was a child born of a virgin. What evidence is there?

'TWAS THE FASHION

What evidence? Do you suppose you could get any positive evidence that would make anyone believe that story today of anybody, no matter who it was?

Child, born of a virgin? There were at least four miraculous births recorded in the Testament. There was Sarah's child, there was Samson, there was John the Baptist, and there was Jesus. Miraculous births were rather a fashionable thing in those days, especially in Rome, where most of the theology was laid out.

Caesar had a miraculous birth, Cicero, Alexander from Macedonia—nobody was in style or great unless he had a miraculous birth. It was a land of miracles.

What evidence is there of it? How much evidence would it require for intelligent people to believe such a story? It wouldn't be possible to bring evidence anywhere in this civilized land today, right under your own noses. Nobody would believe it anyway, and yet some people say that you must believe that without a scintilla of evidence of any sort.

Jesus had brothers and sisters older than Himself. His genealogy by Matthew is traced to his father, Joseph, in the first chapter of Matthew. Read that. What did he do?

Well, now, probably some of his teachings were good. We have heard about the Sermon on the Mount. There isn't a single word contained in the Sermon on the Mount that isn't contained in what is called the Sacred Book of the Jews, long before He lived—not one single thing.

Jesus was an excellent student of Jewish theology, as anybody can tell by reading the Gospels; every bit of it was taken from their books of authority, and He simply said what He had heard of for years and years.

But let's look at some things charged to Him. He walked on the water, Now how does that sound? Do you suppose Jesus walked on the water? Joe Smith tried it when he established the Mormon religion. What evidence have you for that?

He found some of His disciples fishing and they hadn't gotten a bite all day. Jesus said, "Cast your nets down there," and they drew them in full of fish. The East Indians couldn't do better than that. What evidence is there of it?

He was at a performance where there were five thousand people and they were out of food, and He asked them how much they had; five loaves and three fishes, or three fishes and five loaves, or something like that, and He made the five loaves and three fishes feed all the multitude, and they picked up I don't know how many barrels afterward. Think of that.

How does that commend itself to intelligent people, coming from a land of myth and fable as all Asia was, a land of myth and fable and ignorance in the main, and before anybody knew anything about science? And yet that must be believed—and is—to save us from our sins.

What are these sins? What has the human race done that

was so bad, except to eat of the tree of knowledge? Does anybody need to save man from his sins in a miraculous way? It is an absurd piece of theology which they themselves say that you must accept on faith because your reason won't lead you to it. You can't do it that way.

WE MUST DEVELOP REASON

I know the weakness of human reason, other people's reason. I know the weakness of it, but it is all we have, and the only safety of man is to cultivate it and extend his knowledge so that he will be sure to understand life and as many of the mysteries of the universe as he can possibly solve.

Jesus practiced medicine without medicine. Now think of this one. He was traveling along the road and somebody came and told Him there was a sick man in the house and he wanted Him to cure him. How did He do it? Well, there were a lot of hogs out in the front yard and He drove the devils out of the man and cured him, but He drove them into the hogs and they jumped into the sea. Is that a myth or is it true?

If that is true, if you have got to believe that story in order to have your soul saved, you are bound to get rid of your intelligence to save the soul that perhaps doesn't exist at all. You can't believe a thing just because you want to believe it and you can't believe it on very poor evidence. You may believe it because your grandfather told you it was true, but you have got to have some such details.

Did He raise a dead man to life? Why, tens of thousands of dead men and women have been raised to life according to all the stories and all the traditions. Was this the only case? All Europe is filled with miracles of that sort, the Catholic church performing miracles almost to the present time. Does anybody believe it if they use their senses? I say, No. It is impossible to believe it if you use your senses.

Now take the soul. People in this world instinctively like to keep on living. They want to meet their friends again, and all of that. They cling to life. Schopenhauer called it the will to live. I call it the momentum of a going machine. Anything that is going keeps on going for a certain length of time. It is all momentum. What evidence is there that we are alive after we are dead?

But that wasn't the theory of theology. The theory of theology—and it is a part of a creed of practically every Christian church today—is that you die and go down into the earth and you are dead, and when Gabriel comes back to blow his horn, the dust is gathered together and, lo and behold, you appear the same old fellow again and live here on earth!

How many believe it? And yet that is the only idea of immortality there is, and it is in every creed today, I believe.

MATTER INDESTRUCTIBLE

And everything that is in the body and in the man goes into something else, turns into the crucible of nature, goes to make trees and grass and weeds and fruit, and is eaten by all kinds of life, and in that way goes on and on.

Of course, in a sense, nobody dies. The matter that is in me will exist in another form when I am dead. The force that is in me will live in some other kind of force when I am dead. But I will be gone.

That isn't the kind of immortality people want. They want to know that they can recognize Mary Jane in heaven. Don't they? They want to see their brothers and their sisters and their friends in heaven. It isn't possible. We know where our life began; we know where it ends.

We know where every individual life on earth began. It began in a single cell, in the body of our mother, who had some ten thousand of those cells. It was fertilized by a spermatozoan from the body of our father, who had a million of them, any one of which, under certain circumstances, would fertilize a cell.

They multiplied and divided until a child was born. And in old age or accident or disease, they fall apart and the man is done.

AGNOSTIC BECAUSE I MUST REASON

Can you imagine an eternity with one end cut off? Something that began but never ended? We began our immortality at a certain time, when the cell and the spermatozoan conspired to form a human being. We began then. If I am not the product of a spermatozoan and a cell, and if those cells that are unfertilized produce life, and those spermatozoa that fertilized no life were still alive, then I must have ten thousand brothers and sisters on my mother's side and a million on my father's. It is utterly absurd.

I am an agnostic because no man living can form any picture of any God, and you can't believe in an object unless you can form a picture of it. You may believe in the force, but not in the object.

If there is any God in the universe I don't know it. Some people say they know it instinctively. Well, the errors and foolish things that men have known instinctively are so many we can't talk about them.

As a rule, the less a person knows, the surer he is, and he gets it by instinct, and it can't be disputed; for I don't know what is going on in another man's mind. I have no such instinct.

Let me give you just one more idea of a miracle of this Jesus story that has run down through the ages and is not at all the sole property of the Christian.

You remember, when Jesus was born in a manger, according to the story, there came wise men from the east to Jerusalem. And they were led by a star.

Now the closet star to the earth is more than a billion miles away. Think of the star leading three moth-eaten camels to a manger! Can you imagine a star standing over any house?

Can you imagine a star standing over the earth even? What would they say, if they had time? That was a miracle. It came down to the earth.

Well, if any star came that near the earth or anywhere near the earth, it would immediately disarrange the whole solar system. Anybody who can believe those old myths and fables isn't governed by reason.

Charles Darwin

Charles Robert Darwin (1809-1882), through his theory of evolution, has become so powerful an anti-Christian force in Western culture that he is commonly considered a militant foe of religion. Actually he was a rather reluctant foe.

He came to his agnostic position slowly and with many misgivings. He was subject to heavy family pressure in behalf of religious conformity, and when his autobiography was published posthumously, many of his critical phrases about religion were omitted in order to save the feelings of members of his family and other faithful believers.

When Darwin went to Cambridge, he was headed toward Holy Orders. He read with admiration William Paley's *A View of the Evidences of Christianity* and said that "as I did not then in the least doubt the strict and literal truth of every word of the Bible; I soon persuaded myself that our Creed must be fully accepted." Even when he embarked as a naturalist for five years on the *Beagle,* he took along Milton's *Paradise Lost* as his favorite poem and argued with the ship's officers as a defender of the Bible.

He was shocked by the storm of vituperation that followed the publication of *Origin of Species*. At that time he considered himself a theist. A distinguished Protestant clergyman declared that Darwinism was "an attempt to dethrone God," and later Pope Pius IX publicly thanked a writer who "so well refuted the aberrations of Darwinism."

Fortunately we now have Darwin's own story of his religious development complete in *The Autobiography of Charles Darwin,* edited by his granddaughter, Nora Barlow. Permission to quote from the section on religion has been granted kindly by Harcourt Brace Jovanovich.

The complete text reveals how seriously Mrs. Darwin and others modified some of Darwin's most caustic criticisms of orthodoxy by dropping out phrases and whole sentences. For example, the following sentence was completely excised: "I can indeed hardly see how anyone ought to wish Christianity to be true; for if so the plain language of the text seems to show that the men who do not believe, and this would include my Father, Brother and almost all my best friends, will be everlastingly punished." And he added a punch line, which Mrs. Darwin also excised: "And this is damnable doctrine!"

I am reprinting here all those portions of the section called "Religious Beliefs" that were originally censored, indicating in brackets the portions that were removed. It will be seen that although Darwin moved very slowly toward unbelief, he was clearly antagonistic to orthodox Christianity at the end.

—P.B.

De-Censoring Darwin's Religion

During these two years (October 1836 to January 1839) I was led to think much about religion. Whilst on board the *Beagle* I was quite orthodox, and I remember being heartily laughed at by several of the officers (though themselves orthodox) for quoting the Bible as an unanswerable authority on some point of morality. I suppose it was the novelty of the argument that amused them. But I had gradually come, by this time, to see that the Old Testament [from its manifestly false history of the world, with the Tower of Babel, the rainbow as a sign, and so forth, and from its attributing to God the feelings of a revengeful tyrant, was no more to be trusted than the sacred books of the Hindoos, or the beliefs of any barbarian.] The question then continually rose before my mind and would not be banished—Is it credible that if God were now to make a revelation to the Hindoos, would ne permit it to be connected with the belief in Vishnu, Siva, and so on, as Christianity is connected with the Old Testament? This appeared to me utterly incredible.

By further reflecting that the clearest evidence would be requisite to make any sane man believe in the miracles by which

Christianity is supported—that the more we know of the fixed laws of nature the more incredible do miracles become—that the men at that time were ignorant and credulous to a degree almost incomprehensible by us—that the Gospels cannot be proved to have been written simultaneously with the events—that they differ in many important details, far too important as it seemed to me to be admitted as the usual inaccuracies of eyewitnesses; by such reflections as these, which I give not as having the least novelty or value, but as they influenced me, I gradually came to disbelieve in Christianity as a divine revelation. The fact that many false religions have spread over large portions of the earth like wild-fire had some weight with me. [Beautiful as is the morality of the New Testament, it can hardly be denied that its perfection depends in part on the interpretation which we now put in metaphors and allegories.]

But I was very unwilling to give up my belief—I feel sure of this for I can well remember often and often inventing daydreams of old letters between distinguished Romans and manuscripts being discovered at Pompeii or elsewhere which confirmed in the most striking manner all that was written in the Gospels. But I found it more and more difficult, with free scope given to my imagination, to invent evidence which would suffice to convince me. Thus disbelief crept over me at a very slow rate, but was at last complete. The rate was so slow that I felt no distress [and have never since doubted even for a single second that my conclusion was correct. I can indeed hardly see how anyone ought to wish Christianity to be true; for if so the plain language of the text seems to show that the men who do not believe, and this would include my Father, Brother and almost all my best friends, will be everlastingly punished.]

[And this is a damnable doctrine.]

Although I did not think much about the existence of a personal God until a considerably later period of my life, I will here give the vague conclusions to which I have been driven. The old argument of design in nature, as given by Paley, which formerly seemed to me so conclusive, fails now that the law of natural selection has been covered. We can no longer argue that, for instance, the beautiful hinge of a bivalve shell must have been made by an intelligent being, like the hinge of a door by man. There seems to be no more design in the variability of organic beings and in the action of natural selection, than in the course which the wind blows. [Everything in nature is the result of fixed laws.] . . .

But passing over the endless beautiful adaptations which we everywhere meet with, it may be asked how can the generally beneficent arrangement of the world be accounted for? Some writers indeed are so much impressed with the amount of suffering in the world, that they doubt if we look to all sentient beings, whether there is more of misery or of happiness—whether the world as a whole is a good or a bad one. According to my judgment happiness decidedly prevails, though this would be very difficult to prove. If the truth of this conclusion be granted, it harmonises well with the effects which we might expect from natural selection. . . .

That there is much suffering in the world no one disputes. Some have attempted to explain this in reference to man by imagining that it serves for his moral improvement. But the number of men in the world is nothing compared with that of all other sentient beings, and these often suffer greatly without any moral improvement. [A being so powerful and so full of knowledge as a God who could create the universe, is to our finite minds omnipotent and omniscient, and it revolts our understanding to suppose that his benevolence is not unbounded, for what advantage can there be in the sufferings of millions of the lower animals throughout almost endless time?] This very argument from the existence of suffering against the existence of an intelligent first cause seems to me a stong one; whereas, as just remarked, the presence of much suffering agrees well with the view that all organic beings have been developed through variation and natural selection.

At the present day the most usual argument for the existence of an intelligent God is drawn from the deep inward conviction and feelings which are experienced by most persons. [But it cannot be doubted that Hindoos, Mahomadans and others might argue in the same manner and with equal force in favour of the existence of one God, or of many Gods, or as with the Buddists of no God. There are also many barbarian tribes who cannot be said with any truth to believe in what we call God: they believe indeed in spirits or ghosts, and it can be explained, as Tyler and Herbert Spencer have shown, how such a belief would be likely to arise.]

Formerly I was led by feelings such as those just referred to (although I do not think that the religious sentiment was ever strongly developed in me), to the firm conviction of the existence of God, and of the immortality of the soul. In my Journal I wrote that whilst standing in the midst of the grandeur of a Brazilian forest, "it is not possible to give an adequate idea of the higher feelings of wonder, admiration, and devotion which fill and elevate the mind." I well remember my conviction that there is more in man than the mere breath of his body. But now the grandest scenes would not cause any such convictions and feelings to rise in my mind. It may be truly said that I am like a man who has become colour-blind, and the universal belief by men of the existence of redness makes my present loss of perception of not the least value as evidence. This argument would be a valid one if all men of all races had the same inward conviction of the existence of one God; but we know that this is very far from being the case. Therefore I cannot see that such inward convictions and feelings are of any weight as evidence of what really exists. The state of mind which grand scenes formerly excited in me, and which was intimately connected with a belief in God, did not essentially differ from that which is often called the sense of sublimity; and however difficult it may be to explain the genesis of this sense, it can hardly be advanced as an argument for the existence of God, any more that the powerful though vague and similar feelings excited by music.

With respect to immortality, nothing shows me how strong and almost instinctive a belief it is, as the consideration of the view now held by most physicists, namely that the sun with all the planets will in time grow too cold for life, unless indeed some great body dashes into the sun and thus gives it fresh life. Believing as I do that man in the distant future will be a far more perfect creature than he now is, it is an intolerable thought that he and all other sentient beings are doomed to complete annihilation after such long-continued slow progress. To those who fully admit the immortality of the human soul, the destruction of our world will not appear so dreadful.

Another source of conviction in the existence of God, connected with the reason and not with the feelings, impresses me as having much more weight. This follows from the extreme difficulty or rather impossibility of conceiving this immense and wonderful universe, including man with his capacity of looking far backwards and far into futurity, as the result of blind chance or necessity. When thus reflecting, I feel compelled to look to a First Cause having an intelligent mind in some degree analogous to that of man; and I deserve to be called a Theist.

This conclusion was strong in my mind about the time, as far as I can remember, when I wrote the *Origin of Species*; and it is since that time that it has very gradually with many fluctuations become weaker. But then arises the doubt—can the mind of man, which has, as I fully believe, been developed from a mind as low as that possessed by the lowest animal, be trusted when it draws such grand conclusions? [May not these be the result of the connection between cause and effect which strikes us as a necessary one, but probably depends merely on inherited experience? Nor must we overlook the probability of the constant inculcation in a belief in God on the minds of children producing so strong and perhaps an inherited effect on their brains not yet fully developed, that it would be as difficult for them to throw off their belief in God, as for a monkey to throw off its instinctive fear and hatred of a snake.]

I cannot pretend to throw the least light on such abstruse problems. The mystery of the beginning of all things is insoluble by us; and I for one must be content to remain an Agnostic.

[A man who has no assured and ever present belief in the existence of a personal God or a future existence with retribution and a reward, can have for this rule of life, as far as I can see, only to follow those impulses and instincts which are the strongest or which seem to him the best ones. A dog acts in this manner, but he does so blindly. A man, on the other hand, looks forwards and backwards, and compares his various feelings, desires and recollections. He then finds, in accordance with the verdict of all the wisest men, that the highest satisfaction is derived from following certain impulses, namely the social instincts. If he acts for the good of others, he will receive the approbation of his fellow men and gain the love of those with whom he lives; and this latter gain undoubtedly is the highest pleasure on this earth. By degrees it will become intolerable to him to obey his sensuous passions rather than his higher impulses, which when rendered habitual may be almost called instincts. His reason may occasionally tell him to act in opposition to the opinion of others, whose approbation he will then not receive; but he will still have the solid satisfaction of knowing that he has followed his innermost guide or conscience. As for myself I believe that I have acted rightly, in steadily following and devoting my life to science. I feel no remorse from having committed any great sin, but have often and often regretted that I have not done more direct good to my fellow creatures. My sole and poor excuse is much ill-health and my mental constitution, which makes it extremely difficult for me to turn from one subject or occupation to another. I can imagine with high satisfaction giving up my whole time to philanthropy, but not a portion of it; though this world would have been a far better line of conduct.

[Nothing is more remarkable than the spread of skepticism or rationalism during the latter half of my life. Before I was engaged to be married, my father advised me to conceal carefully my doubts, for he said he had known extreme misery thus caused with married persons. Things went on pretty well until the wife or husband became out of health, and then some women suffered miserably by doubting about the salvation of their husbands, thus making them likewise to suffer. My father added that he had known during his whole long life only three women who were skeptics; and it should be remembered that he knew well a multitude of persons and possessed extraordinary power of winning confidence. When I asked him who the three women were, he had to own with respect to one of them, his sister-in-law Kitty Wedgwood, that he had no good evidence, only the vaguest hints, aided by the conviction that so clear-sighted a woman could not be a believer. At the present time, with my small acquaintance, I know (or have known) several married ladies, who believe a very little more than their husbands. My father used to quote an unanswerable argument, by which an old lady, a Mrs. Barlow, who suspected him of unorthodoxy, hoped to convert him: "Doctor, I know that sugar is sweet in my mouth, and I know that my Redeemer liveth."]

Denis Diderot

Of all the leaders of the French Enlightenment none was more important than Denis Diderot (1713-1784). His *Encyclopedia*, whose thirty-five volumes appeared over a period of twenty years, became a kind of literary anchor in the troubled sea of clerical and revolutionary France. He contributed to that *Encyclopedia* 990 articles. In addition he produced a large number of works in the field of philosophy and religion, as well as some fiction.

Educated by the Jesuits and closely associated with a brother who became a priest, Diderot at thirty married a devout Catholic girl of sixteen who had just come from a convent—and he lived unhappily ever after. His own tentative break with Catholicism had come even before this marriage but he never finalized it. Nor did he ever become an official atheist although his closest friend was the atheist, Baron D'Holbach. When he was thirty-three, he was still able to say: "I was born into the Catholic Apostolic and Roman Church and I subscribe to her decisions with all my might."

Whether this was an induced confession is not clear. Diderot lived in constant fear of Catholic censorship and many of his works were placed on the Vatican's *Index of Prohibited Books*. When he was thirty-six, he was imprisoned for several months for writing "in favor of deism and against morality." One of his early works on philosophy was condemned to the flames by the French Parliament. The first two volumes of his *Encyclopedia* were banned for a time as injurious to religion and royal authority although they contained no overt attack on the Church or the leading dogmas of religion.

Diderot was a great opponent of monasticism. One of his most effective works was a novel which he called *The Nun*, which described the convent experiences of a young girl. The novel included a frank account of lesbianism.

I have chosen two brief excerpts from Diderot. The first is a special paragraph, lifted from Cyril Connally's *Previous Convictions*. The second consists of short extracts from Diderot's delightful, rambling letters to his favorite mistress, Mademoiselle Volland; these appeared in Geoffrey Brereton's *French Thought in the Eighteenth Century*, published by David McKay.

—P.B.

Life

To be born in imbecility, in the midst of pain and crisis; to be the plaything of ignorance, error, need, sickness, wickedness, and passions; to return step by step to imbecility, from the time of lisping to that of doting; to live among knaves and charlatans of all kinds; to die between one man who takes your pulse and another who troubles your head; never to know where you come from, why you come and where you are going! That is what is called the most important gift of our parents and of nature. Life.

Missionaries, Atheists, and Marriage

The English, like us, have a mania for converting people. Their missionaries go off into the depths of the forests to take the catechism to the savages.

There was a native chief who said to one of his missionaries: "Brother, look at my head; my hair is quite grey: seriously, do you think you can make a man of my age believe all these stories? But I have three children. Don't address yourself to the oldest; you will make him laugh. Get hold of the little one; you can persuade him of anything you like."

Another misssionary was preaching our holy religion to some different savages. After listening for some time they asked for a question to be put to the missionary about what they would get out of it all. The missionary said to the interpreter: "Tell them that they will be the servants of God." "Not that, please," answered the interpreter to the missionary; "they don't want to be anybody's servants. "Well," said the missionary, "tell them that they will be the children of God." "That will do very well," said the interpreter. And, indeed, the answer pleased the savages very much. . . .

The Christian religion has nearly died out in England; deists are innumerable; there are scarcely any atheists; those there are hide themselves. An atheist and a scoundrel are practically synonymous over there.

The first time that M. Hume found himself at the table of M. de ——, he was seated next to him. I do not know what led the English philosopher to say that he did not believe in atheists, that he had never seen one M. de——said to him, "Count how many we are here." We were eighteen. M. de —— added: "It is not difficult to be able to count you fifteen straight off; the three others don't know what to think about it."

A nation which thinks that it is belief in God and not good law which makes people honest does not seem to me very advanced. I treat the existence of God, in relation to a people, as I do marriage. The one is a state, the other is a notion, excellent for one or two well-constituted minds, but disastrous for the majority.

The indissoluble marriage vow makes, and will always make, nearly as many unhappy people as it does husbands and wives. Faith in God makes, and will always make, nearly as many fanatics as believers. Wherever people acknowledge a God, there is a cult; wherever there is a cult, the natural order of moral duties is upset and morality corrupted. Sooner or later there comes a moment when the idea which prevented the theft of half-a-crown leads to the masssacre of a hundred thousand men.

A fine compensation! Such has been, such is, such will for all time and for all nations be the effect of a doctrine upon which it is impossible to agree and to which people attach more importance than they do to their lives.

John W. Draper

While Charles Darwin and T. H. Huxley were leading the intellectual struggle against Christian orthodoxy in England during the latter part of the nineteenth century, several American scholars were carrying the scientific battle-flags in American universities. They were not as famous as Darwin or Huxley but ultimately they had great influence. The most famous of them was Andrew D. White, first president of Cornell, described elsewhere in this volume. His gigantic exposé of religious fraud, *A History of the Warfare of Science with Theology in Christendom,* was published in 1896.

Another American scholar, a scientist, had written, almost twenty years earlier, a very effective attack on religious superstition under the title *The Conflict Between Religion and Science,* and his name and fame should be rescued from oblivion. He was John W. Draper (1811-1882), professor of chemistry at New York University. Seven years before his death, in 1875 he issued a powerful exposé of orthodoxy at a time when very few academic leaders in America dared to challenge Christian "history."

Draper, in addition to being a noted historian and anticlerical pioneer, was an inventor in the field of photochemistry and a medical doctor. He showed also that he was an advanced biblical critic, and, fortunately for him, his first venture in this field was a resounding success. *The Conflict Between Religion and Science* became an instant bestseller and passed through at least nineteen editions.

Draper's writing centered upon the operations of the Vatican. His revelations of papal forgeries were sensational, and they were generally accepted in the United States, since Draper was already a noted historian. (He was the author of *The History of the Intellectual Development of Europe.*)

Draper expressed his point of view quite frankly in his preface: "The history of Science is not a mere record of isolated discussions; it is a narrative of the conflict of two contending powers, the expansive force of the human intellect on one side, and the compression arising from traditionary faith and human interest on the other."

The following excerpts, describing clerical power in the Middle Ages, are taken from the nineteenth edition of his famous book.

—P.B.

A Scientist Looks at Religious Graft

All over Europe [under Latin Christianity] the great and profitable political offices were filled by ecclesiastics. In every country there was a dual government: 1. That of a local king, represented by a temporal sovereign; 2. That of a foreign king, acknowledging the authority of the pope. This Roman influence was, in the nature of things, superior to the local: it expressed the sovereign will of one man over all the nations of the continent conjointly, and gathered overwhelming power from its compactness and unity. . . .

The ostensible object of papal intrusion was to secure for the different peoples moral well-being; the real object was to obtain large revenues and give support to large bodies of ecclesiastics. The revenues thus extracted were not infrequently many times greater than those passing into the treasury of the local power. Thus, on the occasion of Innocent IV demanding provision to be made for three hundred additional Italian clergy by the Church of England, and that one of his nephews—a mere boy—should have a stall in Lincoln Cathedral, it was found that the sum already annually abstracted by foreign ecclesiastics from England was thrice that which went into the coffers of the king. . . .

An illiterate condition everywhere prevailing gave opportunity for the development of superstition. Europe was full of disgraceful miracles. On all the roads pilgrims were wending their way to shrines of saints, renowned for the cures they had wrought. It had always been the policy of the Church to discourage the physician and his art; he interfered too much with the gifts and profits of the shrines.

For the prevention of diseases, prayers were put up in the churches, but no sanitary measures were resorted to. From cities reeking with putrefying filth it was thought that plague might be stayed by the prayers of the priests; by them rain and dry weather might be secured, and deliverance obtained from the baleful influence of eclipses and comets. But when Halley's comet came in 1456, so tremendous was its apparition that it was necessary for the pope himself to interfere. He exorcised and expelled it from the skies. It slunk away into the abysses of space, terror-stricken by the maledictions of Calixtus III, and did not venture back for seventy-five years! . . .

To the medical efficacy of shrines must be added that of special relics. These were sometimes of the most extraordinary kind. There were several abbeys that possessed our Savior's crown of thorns. Eleven had the lance that had pierced his side. If any person was adventurous enough to suggest that these could not all be authentic, he would have been denounced as an atheist.

During the holy wars the Templar Knights had driven a profitable commerce by bringing from Jerusalem to the crusading armies bottles of the milk of the Blessed Virgin, which they sold for enormous sums; these bottles were preserved with pious care in many of the great religious establishments. But perhaps none of these impostures surpassed in audacity that offered by a monastery in Jerusalem, which presented to the beholder one of the fingers of the Holy Ghost! . . .

Until the beginning of the ninth century there was no change in the constitution of the Roman Church. But about 845 the Isidorian Decretals were fabricated in the west of Gaul—a forgery containing about one hundred pretended decrees of the early popes, together with certain spurious writings of other church dignitaries and acts of synods. This forgery produced an immense extension of the papal power; it displaced the old system of church government, divesting it of the republican attributes it had possessed and transforming it into an absolute monarchy. . . .

Another fiction concocted in Rome in the eighth century led to important consequences. It feigned that the Emperor Constantine, in gratitude for his cure from leprosy, and baptism by Pope Sylvester, has bestowed Italy and the western provinces on the pope, and that, in token of his subordination, he had served the pope as his groom, and led his horse some distance. This forgery was intended to work on the Frankish kings, to impress them with a correct idea of their inferiority, and to show that, in the territorial concessions they made to the Church, they are not giving but only restoring what rightfully belonged to it.

The most potent instrument of the new papal system was Gratian's Decretum, which was issued about the middle of the twelfth century. It was a mass of fabrications. It made the whole Christian world, through the papacy, the domain of the Italian clergy. It inculcated that it is lawful to constrain men to goodness, to torture and to execute heretics, and to confiscate their property; that to kill an excommunicated person is not murder, that the pope in his unlimited superiority to all laws stands on an equality with the Son of God!

Felix Frankfurter

Felix Frankfurter (1882-1965) described himself as a "reverent agnostic" and "a believing unbeliever." But his doubts did not extend to the Constitution of the United States, and his views of that Constitution did much to shape its interpretation by his fellow justices on the Supreme Court. Frankfurter was a passionate advocate of constitutional religious freedom and the American policy of church-state separation. Also, although he had abandoned formal religious Judaism, he had helped to organize and sustain the Zionist movement.

Born in Vienna, he was brought to this country as an infant by his parents and educated in the public schools of New York. Then he was graduated with honors from New York City College and Harvard Law School. After service in many public positions, he became Harvard's most noted law professor and perhaps the most influential adviser to Franklin Roosevelt. Fighting for Sacco and Vanzetti and against the Palmer red raids of 1919-20, he still retained enough respectability to move to the Supreme Court in 1939. He served on that Court for twenty-three years, becoming the "professor" of that institution, particularly on constitutional law.

Two famous cases involving religion illustrate the depth and range of his thinking on religion and the state. One was the flag salute (Gobitis) case of 1940 in which, speaking for the majority of the Court, he held that the government had the right to expel the children of Jehovah's Witnesses from public schools for refusing to salute the American flag on religious grounds. Frankfurter held that religion should not be used as a shield in such a situation.

Many people did not agree with Frankfurter in this decision, and soon a majority of his own associates on the Court shifted positions and voted with the Witnesses' children. Frankfurter refused to budge on this issue even in defeat, and so he acquired a reputation as a religious-patriotic stickler. But he was far from being a conventional patriot; he simply felt that when "the conscience of the individual collides with the felt necessities of society," the will of society, as expressed by democratic legislative power, should prevail. Behind his reasoning, also was the fear of too much judge-made law.

Frankfurter also had a tremendous loyalty to the American concept of free public education, particularly education without religious bias. This loyalty was the basis of his greatest Court decision, an assenting decision in the McCollum case outlawing religious instruction in Illinois public schools. In that case Frankfurter gave a new substance and glory to the First Amendment: "Congress shall make no law respecting an establishment of religion, or prohibiting the free exercise thereof." That opinion has fortified and helped to exalt the American public school as a religiously neutral institution. I have chosen to quote large sections of that opinion below—in the case of *McCollum* v. *Board of Education*, 333 U.S. 203.

—P.B.

McCollum v.
Board of Education

Illinois has here authorized the commingling of sectarian with secular instruction in the public schools. The Constitution of the United States forbids this.

This case, in the light of the Everson decision, demonstrates anew that the mere formulation of a relevant Constitutional principle is the beginning of the solution of a problem, not its answer. This is so because the meaning of a spacious conception like that of the separation of church from state is unfolded as appeal is made to the principle from case to case. We are all agreed that the First and the Fourteenth Amendments have a secular reach far more penetrating in the conduct of government than merely to forbid an "established church." But agreement, in the abstract, that the First Amendment was designed to erect a "wall of separation between church and state," does not preclude a clash of views as to what the wall separates. Involved is not only the

Constitutional principle but the implications of judicial review in its enforcement. Accommodation of legislative freedom and Constitutional limitations upon that freedom cannot be achieved by a mere phrase. We cannot illuminatingly apply the "wall-of-separation" metaphor until we have considered the relevant history of religious education in America, the place of the "released time" movement in that history, and its precise manifestation in the case before us.

To understand the particular program now before us as a conscientious attempt to accommodate the allowable functions of government and the special concerns of the church within the framework of our Constitution and with due regard to the kind of society for which it was designed, we must put this Champaign program of 1940 in its historic setting.

Traditionally, organized education in the Western world was church education. It could hardly be otherwise when the education of children was primarily study of the Word and the ways of God. Even in the Protestant countries, where there was a less close identification of church and state, the basis of education was largely the Bible, and its chief purpose inculcation of piety. To the extent that the state intervened, it used its authority to further aims of the church.

The emigrants who came to these shores brought this view of education with them. Colonial schools certainly started with a religious orientation. When the common problems of the early settlers of the Massachusetts Bay Colony revealed the need for common schools, the object was the defeat of "one chief project of that old deluder, Satan, to keep men from the knowledge of the Scriptures." . . .

The evolution of colonial education, largely in the service of religion, into the public school system of today is the story of changing conceptions regarding the American democratic society, of the functions of state-maintained education in such a society and of the role therein of the free exercise of religion by the people. The modern public school derived from a philosophy of freedom reflected in the First Amendment. . . .

As the momentum for popular education increased and in turn evoked strong claims for state support of religious education, contests not unlike that which in Virginia had produced Madison's Remonstrance appeared in various forms in other states. New York and Massachusetts provide famous chapters in the history that established dissociation of religious teaching from state-maintained schools. In New York, the rise of the common schools led, despite fierce sectarian opposition, to the barring of tax funds to church schools, and later to any school in which sectarian doctrine was taught. In Massachusetts, largely through the efforts of Horace Mann, all sectarian teachings were barred from the common school to save it from being rent by denominational conflict. The upshot of these controversies, often long and fierce, is fairly summarized by saying that long before the Fourteenth Amendment subjected the states to new limitations, the prohibition of furtherance by the state of religious instruction became the guiding principle, in law and feeling, of the American people. . . .

It is pertinent to remind that the establishment of this principle of separation in the field of education was not due to any decline in the religious beliefs of the people. Horace Mann was a devout Christian, and the deep religious feeling of James Madison is stamped upon the Remonstrance. The secular public school did not imply indifference to the basic role of religion in the life of the people, nor rejection of religious education as a means of fostering it. The claims of religion were not minimized by refusing to make the public schools agencies for their assertion.

The nonsectarian or secular public school was the means of reconciling freedom in general with religious freedom. The sharp confinement of the public schools to secular education was a recognition of the need of a democratic society to educate its children, insofar as the state undertook to do so, in an atmosphere free from pressures in a realm in which pressures are most resisted and where bitterly engendered. Designed to serve as perhaps the most powerful agency for promoting cohesion among a heterogeneous democratic people, the public school must keep scrupulously free from entanglement in the strife of sects.

The preservation of the community from division conflicts, of government from irreconcilable pressures by religious groups, of religion from censorship and coercion however subtly exercised, requires strict confinement of the state to instruction other than religious, leaving to the individual's church and home, indoctrination in the faith of his choice. . . .

The extent to which this principle was deemed a presupposition of our Constitutional system is strikingly illustrated by the fact that every state admitted into the Union since 1876 was compelled by Congress to write into its constitution a requirement that it maintain a school system "free from sectarian control." . . .

How does "released time" operate in Champaign? Public school teachers distribute to their pupils cards supplied by church groups, so that the parents may indicate whether they desire religious instruction for their children. For those desiring it, religious classes are conducted in the regular classrooms of the public schools by teachers of religion paid by the churches and appointed by them, but, as the state court found, "subject to the approval and supervision of the superintendent."

The courses do not profess to give secular instruction in subjects concerning religion. Their candid purpose is sectarian teaching. While a child can go to any of the religious classes offered, a particular sect wishing a teacher for its devotees requires the permission of the school superintendent "who in turn will determine whether or not it is practical for said group to teach in said school system." If no provision is made for religious instruction in the particular faith of a child, or if for other reasons the child is not enrolled in any of the offered classes, he is required to attend a regular school class, or a study period during which he is often left to his own devices. Reports of attendance in the religious classes are submitted by the religious instructor to the school authorities, and the child who fails to attend is presumably deemed a truant.

Religious education so conducted on school time and property is patently woven into the working scheme of the school. The Champaign arrangement thus presents powerful elements of inherent pressure by the school system in the interest of religious sects. The fact that this power has not been used to discriminate is beside the point. Separation is a requirement to abstain from fusing functions of government and of religious sects, not merely to treat them all equally. That a child is offered an alternative may reduce the constraint; it does not eliminate the operation of influence by the school in matters sacred to conscience and outside the school's domain. The law of imitation operates, and nonconformity is not an outstanding characteristic of children. The result is an obvious pressure upon children to attend. . . .

We find that the basic Constitutional principle of absolute separation was violated when the State of Illinois, speaking through its Supreme Court, sustained the school authorities of Champaign in sponsoring and effectively furthering religious beliefs by its educational arrangement.

Separation means separation, not something less. Jefferson's metaphor in describing the relation between church and state speaks of a "wall of separation," not of a fine line easily overstepped. The public school is at once the symbol of our democracy and the most pervasive means for promoting our common destiny. In no activity of the state is it more vital to keep out divisive forces than in its schools, to avoid confusing, not to say fusing, what the Constitution sought to keep strictly apart. "The great American principle of eternal separation"—Elihu Root's phrase bears repetition—is one of the vital reliances of our Constitutional system for assuring unities among our people stronger than our diversities. It is the Court's duty to enforce this principle in its full integrity.

We renew our conviction that "we have staked the very existence of our country on the faith that complete separation between the state and religion is best for the state and best for religion."

Francis Galton

Sir Francis Galton (1822-1911) was one of the great scientists of his time, author of *Hereditary Genius*, grandson of Erasmus Darwin, and cousin of Charles Darwin. His studies in heredity and color blindness were notable as was his sense of humor.

It was this latter trait which inspired him to write one of the most famous magazine articles of the nineteenth century on "Statistical Inquiries Into the Efficacy of Prayer." He must have become annoyed by the stupid and bitter clerical attacks on his cousin Charles for propounding the theory of evolution. It was an unusual thing for a great scientist to take issue with ordinary religious superstitions, but Galton decided to try his hand at subtle satire. He solemnly marshalled the reasons why orthodox Christian prayer did not seem to pay off, and he published his "research" in one of England's most respectable journals, *The Fortnightly Review* of August 1, 1872. The article was a great success, partly because of its subtle side-attack on the whole system of upper class snobbery in England. It is scarcely necessary to say that Galton's challenge to examine the efficacy of prayer was never accepted by the clergy.

—P.B.

Statistical Inquiries Into the Efficacy of Prayer

An eminent authority has recently published a challenge to test the efficacy of prayer by actual experiment. I have been induced through reading this, to prepare the following memoir for publication. . . .

The efficacy of prayer seems to me a simple, as it is a perfectly appropriate and legitimate, subject of scientific inquiry. Whether prayer is efficacious or not, in any given sense, is a matter of fact on which each man must form an opinion for himself. His decision will be based upon data more or less justly handled, according to his education and habits. An unscientific reasoner will be guided by a confused recollection of crude experience. A scientific reasoner will scrutinise each separate experience before he admits it as evidence, and will compare all the cases he has selected on a methodical system.

The doctrine commonly preached by the clergy is well expressed in the most recent, and by far the most temperate and learned of theological encyclopaedias, namely, "Smith's Dictionary of the Bible." The article on "Prayer," written by the Rev. Dr. Barry, states as follows: "Its real objective efficacy . . . is both implied and expressed [in Scripture] in the plainest terms. . . . We are encouraged to ask special blessings, both spiritual and temporal, in hopes that thus, and thus only, we may obtain them. . . . It would seem the intention of Holy Scripture to encourage all prayer, more especially intercession, in all relations and for all righteous objects." . . .

The phrases of our Church service amply countenance this view; and if we look to the practice of the opposed sections of the religious world, we find them consistent in maintaining it. The so-called "Low Church" notoriously places absolute belief in special providences accorded to pious prayer. This is testified by the biographies of its members, the journals of its missionaries, and the "united prayer-meetings" of the present day. The Roman Catholics offer religious vows to avert danger; they make pilgrimages to shrines; they hang votive offerings and pictorial representations, sometimes by thousands, in their churches, of fatal accidents averted by the manifest interference of a solicited saint.

The principles are broad and simple upon which our inquiry into the efficacy of prayer must be established. We must gather cases for statistical comparison, in which the same object is keenly pursued by two classes similar in their physical, but opposite in their spiritual state; the one class being prayerful, the other materialistic. Prudent pious people must be compared with prudent materialistic people, and not with the imprudent nor the vicious. Secondly, we have no regard, in this inquiry, to the course by which the answer to prayers may be supposed to operate. We simply look to the final result—whether those who pray attain their objects more frequently than those who do not pray, but who live in all other respects under similar conditions. Let us now apply our principles to different cases.

A rapid recovery from disease may be conceived to depend on many causes besides the reparative power of the patient's constitution. A miraculous quelling of the disease may be one of these causes; another is the skill of the physician, or of the nurse; another is the care that the patient takes of himself. In our inquiry, whether prayerful people recover more rapidly than others under similar circumstances, we need not complicate the question by endeavoring to learn the channel through which the patient's prayer may have reached its fulfilment. It is foreign to our present purpose to ask if there be any signs of a miraculous quelling of the disease, or if, through the grace of God, the physician had showed unusual wisdom, or the nurse or the patient unusual discretion. We simply look to the main issue—do sick persons who pray, or are prayed for, recover on the average more rapidly than others?

It appears that, in all countries and in all creeds, the priests urge the patient to pray for his own recovery, and the patient's friends to aid him with their prayers; but that the doctors make no account whatever of their spiritual agencies, unless the office of priest and medical man be combined in the same individual. The medical works of modern Europe teem with records of individual illnesses and of broad averages of disease, but I have been able to discover hardly any instance in which a medical man of any repute has attributed recovery to the influence of prayer.

Those who may wish to pursue these inquiries upon the effect of prayers for the restoration of health could obtain abundant materials from hospital cases, and in a different way from that proposed in the challenge to which I referred at the beginning of these pages. There are many common maladies whose course is so thoroughly well understood as to admit of accurate tables of probability being constructed for their duration and result. Such are fractures and amputations. Now it would be perfectly practicable to select out of the patients at different hospitals under treatment for fractures and amputations two considerable groups; the one consisting of markedly religious and piously befriended individuals, the other of those who were remarkably cold-hearted and neglected. An honest comparison of their respective periods of treatment and the results would manifest a distinct proof of the efficacy of prayer, if it existed to even a minute fraction of the amount that religious teachers exhort us to believe.

An inquiry of a somewhat similar nature may be made into the longevity of persons whose lives are prayed for; also that of the praying classes generally; and in both these cases we can easily obtain statistical facts. The public prayer for the sovereign of every state, Protestant and Catholic, is and has been in the spirit of our own, "Grant her in health long to live." Now, as a simple matter of fact, has this prayer any efficacy? There is a memoir by Dr. Guy, in the *Journal of the Statistical Society* (vol. xxii, p. 355), in which he compares the mean age of sovereigns with that of other classes of persons. His results are expressed in the table below. The sovereigns are literally the shortest lived of all who have the advantage of affluence. The prayer has therefore no efficacy, unless the very questionable hypothesis be raised, that the conditions of royal life may naturally be yet more fatal, and that their influence is partly, though incompletely, neutralised by the effects of public prayers.

It will be seen that the same findings collate the longevity of clergy, lawyers, and medical men. We are justified in considering the clergy to be a far more prayerful class than either of the other two. It is their profession to pray, and they have the practice of offering morning and evening family prayers in addition to their private devotions. A reference to any of the numerous published collections of family prayers will show that they are full of petitions for temporal benefits. We do not, however, find that the clergy are in any way more long lived in consequence. It is true that the clergy, as a whole, show a life-value of 69-49, as against 68-14 for the lawyers, and 67-31 for the medical men; but the easy country life and family repose of so many of the clergy are obvious sanatory conditions in their favour. This difference is reversed when the comparison is made between distinguished members of the three classes—that is to say, between persons of sufficient note to have had their lives recorded in a biographical dictionary. When we examine this category, the value of life among the clergy, lawyers, and medical men is as 66-42, 66-51, and 67-04 respectively, the clergy being the shortest lived of the three. Hence the prayers of the clergy for protection against the perils and dangers of the night, for protection during the day, and for recovery from sickness, appear to be futile in result.

In my work on "Hereditary Genius," and in the chapter on "Divines," I have worked out the subject with some minuteness on other data, but with precisely the same result. I show that the divines are not specially favoured in those worldly matters for which they naturally pray, but rather the contrary, a fact which I ascribe in part to their having, as a class, indifferent constitutional vigour.

A further inquiry may be made into the duration of life among missionaries. We should lay greater stress upon their mortality than upon that of the clergy, because the laudable object of a missionary's career is rendered almost nugatory by his early death. A man goes, say, to a tropical climate, in the prime of manhood, who has the probability of many years of useful life before him, had he remained at home. He has the certainty of being able to accomplish sterling good as a missionary, if he should live long enough to learn the language and habits of the country. In the interval he is almost useless. Yet the painful experience of many years shows only too clearly that the missionary is not supernaturally endowed with health. One missionary after another dies shortly after his arrival.

The efficacy of prayer may yet further be tested by inquiry into the proportion of deaths at the time of birth among the children of the praying and the non-praying classes. The solicitude of parents is so powerfully directed towards the safety of their expected offspring as to leave no room to doubt that pious parents pray fervently for it, especially as death before baptism is considered a most serious evil by many Christians. However, the distribution of still-births appears wholly unaffected by piety. The proportion of the still-births published in the *Record* newspaper and in the *Times* was found to bear an identical relation to the total number of deaths. . . .

To proceed with our inquiry, we may ask,—Is a bank or other commercial undertaking more secure when devout men are among its shareholders,—or when the funds of pious people, or charities, or of religious bodies are deposited in its keeping, or when its proceedings are opened with prayer, as was the case with the disastrous Royal British Bank? It is impossible to say yes. There are far too many sad experiences of the contrary.

Mean Age attained by Males of various classes who had survived their 30th Year, from 1758 to 1843. Deaths by Accident or Violence are excluded.

			Average	Eminent Men
Members of Royal houses	97	in number	64-04	
Clergy	945	"	69-49	66-42
Lawyers	294	"	68-14	66-51
Medical Profession	244	"	67-31	67-07
English aristocracy	1,179	"	67-31	
Gentry	1,632	"	70-22	
Trade and commerce	513	"	68-74	
Officers in the Royal Navy	366	"	68-40	
English literature and science	395	"	67-55	65-22
Officers of the Army	569	"	67-07	
Fine Arts	239	"	65-96	64-74

E. Haldeman-Julius

I suppose that the two most successful American propagandists in the field of religion in this century have been Billy Graham and E. Haldeman-Julius, Graham for and Haldeman-Julius against. Graham has achieved international fame but Haldeman-Julius is almost forgotten in spite of the fact that he produced several hundred million Little Blue Books primarily designed to foster free thought. (I am glad to note that William Ryan is writing a biography of Haldeman-Julius.)

Emanuel Haldeman-Julius (1889-1951), son of a Jewish immigrant, was born Emanuel Julius but adopted a new and hyphenated name when he married into a banking family. His new family status made it possible for him to buy out a flourishing radical newspaper in Girard, Kansas, the *Appeal to Reason*. He had been an experienced New York journalist with a socialist outlook, and he proceeded to make the *Appeal to Reason* and its associated publishing ventures into a gigantic success. He was able to enlist for his Little Blue Books some of the world's most popular and competent writers, including Will Durant, Clarence Darrow and Bertrand Russell. His most prolific contributor was the famous, Irish ex-priest, Joseph McCabe. He sold about two hundred million copies of the Little Blue Books in the first twenty years, and they generally sold at five cents each.

Once when he was asked to explain himself to a reader, he replied:

> I've never posed as a savior of humanity. My position is clear and simple. It happens that I am just a small-town printer who thinks ideas are important. I could publish trash, like any other commercial publisher, but this wouldn't give me any satisfaction. . . . honesty makes me confess that it might happen that I couldn't even pay expenses if I followed the lead of the publishers of the pulps or the confession magazines, à la McFadden, so it's perhaps additional proof of enlightened selfishness when I go out of my way to issue such literary matter as I consider to be a real value and permanent significance. I'd rather publish one book by a Joseph McCabe than a thousand tomes by Harold Bell Wright.

I have chosen to reprint a few typical questions and answers from Haldeman-Julius's magazine of that name. His answers show the style and directness which his writing exemplified. His conclusion that "religion is all bad" shocked many of his readers—but it sold more Little Blue Books.

—P.B.

The Mental Disease Called Religion

I dislike becoming personal, Mr. Haldeman-Julius, but some of the answers in The Freeman *almost compel me to ask if you entirely deny the existence of a Heavenly Father or merely fight the bad features of certain religious denominations.*

I dislike to disappoint my reader, but it happens there's some foundation to his suspicions. While I don't go around denying the existence of a Heavenly Father or a Celestial Mama, I do hint now and then that I believe those who support such theistic notions aren't able to buttress their opinions with the slightest show of evidence.

I thought it would be better to let this reader have the cold, bitter truth now, instead of waiting until the terrible truth about me creeps on him like a cancer and strikes him down in life's young morning. And while I am exposing my intellectual sins and cultural diseases, let me correct my reader's suggestion that I "merely fight features of certain religious denominations."

That's too mealy-mouth to suit my robust nature. To begin with, I don't go after "certain bad features" at all, because it's my measured opinion—after thirty-five years of study—that religion is all bad, without a single good feature. And, of course, that means I don't go gunning after "certain religious denominations" but send my gas bombs into the whole kit and kaboodle. It's part of my philosophy that the world would be a better place for all of us if we managed to get rid of the mental disease called religion.

How did Adam get the words with which to give names to all the animals?

God, who was exceptionally busy at the time, gave the job of naming the animals to Adam. They were marched before him, in a long row, and he looked each one over and thought of the name that would fit the beast. Where he got so many words shouldn't cause wonder, considering he had God right at his elbow to egg him on. For example, when the hog was brought before Adam to be named, how simple it is to assume that since the beast behaved like a hog it would be right smart to call him by that name.

Can you tell me how many cases of incest are described in the Bible?

1. Lot with his elder daughter, Genesis 19:33
2. Lot with his younger daughter, Genesis 19:35
3. Abraham with his half sister, Genesis 20:12
4. Nahor with his niece, Genesis 11:27, 20
5. Reuben with his father's concubine, Genesis 35:22, 49:4
6. Amram with his aunt, Exodus 6:20
7. Judah with his daughter-in-law, Genesis 38:16-18
8. Amnon with his sister, Second Samuel 13:2, 14
9.-18. Absalom with his father's 10 concubines, Second Samuel 15:16; 16:21-22
19. Herod with his sister-in-law, Mark 6:17-18
    See also Amos 2:7 and First Corinthians 5:1
    And how about Cain (Genesis 4:17) and Seth (Genesis 4:26)?

Is there not a psychological similarity between the idea of God and that of Santa Claus?

There is, without a doubt. It's the impulse to get favors, to beg for gifts, to get something for nothing. It's a pleasant game. One asks God for a new car, or a new jock-strap, or even a new box of Kotex. It doesn't hurt to ask. . . .

George Jacob Holyoake

George Jacob Holyoake was, according to his own description of himself, the last Englishman to be tried by a jury for the crime of atheism. His address to the jury in that trial, in May 1842, is one of the relatively unknown classics of English intellectual history.

Although Holyoake was described as a yeoman, he was a rather sophisticated yeoman, a professional socialist lecturer, a disciple of Robert Owen, and editor of a small free-thought journal, the *Oracle of Reason*. According to police statements, Holyoake, speaking in the parish of Cheltenham, Gloucestershire, "wickedly and profanely uttered, made use of and proclaimed, in the presence of a public assembly of men, women and children . . . certain impious and blasphemous words against God and concerning the Christian religion, to wit 'That he was of no religion at all and that he did not believe that there was such a thing as a God, and that if he could have his way he would place the Deity on half-pay, as the government of this country did the subaltern officers [of the army].'" This, said the authorities, "was against the peace of our lady the Queen, her crown and dignity."

When arraigned before a committing magistrate, Holyoake's accuser declared: "I attend to prefer the charge of blasphemy, and I shall take my stand on the common unwritten law of the land. . . . Any person who denies the existence or providence of God is guilty of blasphemy, and the law has annexed to that offence imprisonment, corporal punishment, and fine." When Holyoake attempted to discuss his case with the magistrate, that official declared: "We refuse to hold an argument with a man professing the abominable principle of denying the existence of a Supreme Being."

When Holyoake finally appeared for trial before Justice Erskine, the judge was somewhat embarrassed by the sweeping implications of the charge. "An honest man," said Erskine, "speaking his opinions decently, is entitled to do so . . . if it be done seriously and decently all men are at liberty to state opinions." But Holyoake had sought to bring "Almighty

God, the Holy Scriptures, and the Christian religion into disbelief and contempt among the people of this kingdom by adding that "I would have the Deity serve as they served the subalterns, place him on half-pay.'" So Holyoake was tried for "contempt" as well as blasphemy. Erskine, in his charge to the jury, declared that "without religion there is no morality," and that "if men will entertain sentiments opposed to the religion of the state, we require that they shall express them reverently."

Holyoake made a very strenuous defense, insisting on acting as his own counsel and holding the floor at one time for eleven hours. But his case was doomed, partly because public opinion had been inflamed against dissidents by a recent attempt to assassinate Queen Victoria. Holyoake was quickly found guilty and sent to a common jail for six months, where he led a protest against the starvation diet prescribed for common prisoners at that time—gruel, bread, and potatoes. Later the public attitude toward him changed, and he became mildly popular.

I have condensed excerpts from the 1859 edition of Holyoake's small book, the *History of the Last Trial by Jury for Atheism in England.*
—P.B.

An Atheist's Speech to the Jury

I am unaccustomed to address a jury, and I hope to avoid the charge of presumption or dogmatism. I have no wish to offend the prejudices of any man in this court, and have no interest in so doing. . . . But while I profess respect for your opinions, I must entertain some of my own.

There are those here who think religion proper, and that it alone can lead to general happiness. I do not, and I have had the same means of judging. You say your feelings are insulted, your opinions outraged, but what of mine? Mine, however honest, are rendered liable to punishment. . . . Christianity claims what she does not allow, although she says all men are brothers. . . .

I am not a bigot. I do not assume that I alone am right; nor did I speak of Deity, declaring dramatically his nonexistence. I spoke only of my own disbelief in such an existence. Of all isms I think dogmatism the worst.

I do not judge other men by the agreement of their opinions with my own. I believe you consider Christianity a benefit. I regret that I feel it is not so, and I claim the privilege of saying what is true to me. . . . Strong prejudice exists against me as being a Socialist. But this I have learned from Socialism, that there can be no public or private virtue unless the foundation of action is the practice of truth.

It is laid down by the common law that a person denying the existence of a God is a blasphemer. . . . It has not been shown that I did this. I merely stated my disbelief—and disbelief is not included by the law. . . .

My only crime has been the discharge of what I considered a duty. For my difference in opinion with you upon the question of Deity, I offer no apology. I have made no contract to think as you do, and I owe you no obligation to do it. If I commanded you to abjure your belief you would disregard it as impertinence, and if you punish me for not abjuring mine, how will you reconcile it with doing as you would wish to be done unto? . . . If I have said that religious revenues should be reduced one half, I spoke only the dictate of humanity at this season of national suffering. Surely it is not blasphemous to argue that human misery should be alleviated at the expense of spiritual pride.

I ask not equal rights with yourselves. You, as Christians, can imprison those who differ from you. I do not offend your pride by asking to be admitted your equals here. I desire not such privileges. I claim merely the right to speak my convictions: to show a man the right path when I think he takes the wrong one. . . .

Gentlemen . . . I best prefer appealing to you as honest men, in the spirit of my own reasoning and thinking; as men with an eye to the improvement of mankind who would break the unjust shackles that bind them, who would discard prejudice in order to be just, who will not condemn me because I am not rich, and who listen to humanity rather than bigotry, and respect truthfulness wherever you may find it. I believe that in every honest heart there is a sense of rectitude that rises superior to creeds, that respects all virtue and protects all truth. . . . To this feeling, gentlemen, only do I appeal, and by this verdict I am willing to abide.

Julian Huxley

Julian Sorrell Huxley, who died in 1975 at the age of eighty-seven, may well go down in history as the most eminent humanist for our time. Because of his fame on both sides of the Atlantic—he was the first director general of Unesco, the most prominent English popularizer of science, a famous news broadcaster, and a frequent lecturer in American universities—he probably deserves to be known as Mr. World Humanist of our era. Not the least of his accomplishments was his popularization of the humanist label as one of dignity, devotion, and scholarship.

I never knew him well, although he once spent a week in our home. The two things I remember best from that week are, first, his remarkably detailed knowledge of the life of animals and birds, and second, his warm defense of his brother Aldous. I had said something disparaging about Aldous' dip into the misty regions of illusion and hallucination—Aldous had once said, "We are all on the way to an existential religion of mysticism." To my surprise Julian defended his brother warmly as an important scientific experimenter. After Aldous' death, Julian declared of his brother that "he will go down in history as the greatest humanist of our perplexed era."

Actually it is Julian himself who will go down as the most versatile humanist missionary of our perplexed era. Although he lacked the dramatic forensic powers of his grandfather, T. H. Huxley, and the writing skills of his brother Aldous, he was an amazingly versatile person who never ran away from a good fight in the field of religious controversy. He rejected all forms of religious orthodoxy, Christian and otherwise, and declared that "man's destiny is to make possible a maximum fulfillment for the greatest number of human beings. This is the only goal at which we must aim." To attain that fulfillment, he wanted humanism to use all physical and intellectual resources. His own brilliant versatility was demonstrated in his youth when he took a first in zoology at Oxford and simultaneously won Oxford's highest poetry prize.

He came under heavy fire from Roman Catholicism and from Protestant orthodoxy during the period of his leadership of Unesco, partly because of his advanced views on sex and genetics. He challenged the whole conventional breeding system of our era and championed world-wide birth control.

I have chosen to reprint two short passages from Julian Huxley's work, with the kind permission of Harper and Row, his publisher. The first is from his early work *Religion Without Revelation*, a book that may still stand as his most significant, and the second is from his later *New Bottles for New Wine*.

—P.B.

Religion Without Revelation

In the first place, I believe, not that there *is* nothing, for that I do not know, but that we quite assuredly at present *know* nothing beyond this world and natural experience. A personal God, be he Jehovah, or Allah, or Apollo, or Amon-Ra, or without name but simply God, I *know* nothing of. What is more, I am not merely agnostic on the subject. It seems to me quite clear that the idea of personality in God or in any supernatural being or beings has been put there by man, put into and round a perfectly real conception which we might continue to call God if the word had not acquired by a long association the implication of a personal being, and therefore I disbelieve in a personal God in any sense in which that phrase is ordinarily used.

For similar reasons, I disbelieve in the existence of Heaven or Hell in any conventional Christian sense. As for any pretended knowledge about the Last Judgment or the condition of existence in Purgatory, it could be disregarded as what it is, mythology from racial childhood, and left to die a natural death, if it did not require to be attacked as the frequent cause of unfortunate prac-tical effects, such as causing believers to pay money to priests for the supposed benefit of souls in the other world. . . .

[Some] believe that their standard of conduct need not be changed, but that they can ensure salvation in another world by special or additional observances or beliefs or offerings. This again I believe not only to involve a false antithesis but to be a denial of the highest religion. More than two thousand years ago the psalmist said that salvation required no propitiatory rites based on crude and anthropomorphic ideas of God; for the acceptable sacrifice is a broken and contrite heart. The Christian world is supposed to believe this, but it, or the great bulk of it, still prefers to stick to what is essentially a magical view of the miraculous efficacy of formulae, or of relics, or the invocation of saints, or of self-deprivation or of prayers, or rites such as absolution by a priest.

Transhumanism

As a result of a thousand million years of evolution, the universe is becoming conscious of itself, able to understand something of its past history and its possible future. This cosmic self-awareness is being realized in one tiny fragment of the universe— in a few of us human beings. . . . Meanwhile do not let us forget that the human species is as radically different from any of the microscopic single-celled animals that lived a thousand million years ago as they were from a fragment of stone or metal.

The new understanding of the universe has come about through the new knowledge amassed in the last hundred years— by psychologists, biologists, and other scientists, by archeologists, anthropologists, and historians. It has defined man's responsibility and destiny—to be an agent for the rest of the world in the job of realizing its inherent potentialities as fully as possible. It is as if man had been suddenly appointed managing director of the biggest business of all, the business of evolution. . . .

The human species can, if it wishes, transcend itself—not just sporadically, an individual here in one way, an individual there in another way, but in its entirety, as humanity. We need a name for this new belief. Perhaps *transhumanism* will serve; man remaining man, but transcending himself, by realizing new possibilities of and for his human nature.

"I believe in transhumanism"; once there are enough people who can truly say that, the human species will be on the threshold of a new kind of existence, as different from ours as ours is from that of the Peking man. It will at last be consciously fulfilling its real destiny.

T. H. Huxley

Thomas Henry Huxley (1825-1895), inventor of the word *agnosticism*, was England's most scholarly foe of orthodox Christianity during the latter part of the nineteenth century. Best known for his defense of the theory of evolution—he was nicknamed "Darwin's bulldog"—he became both a great scientist and a great essayist by sheer industry. With only two years of formal schooling, he outranked all the products of Oxford and Cambridge as an original scholar.

During the last fifteen years of his life he frequently engaged in written and spoken debates on religion with clerics and politicians, his most noted opponents being William Gladstone and Samuel Wilberforce, bishop of Oxford, known as "Soapy Sam." It was Wilberforce, who in the course of a debate inquired blandly whether Huxley traced his gorilla heritage from his grandfather or his grandmother. To which Huxley replied: "I should feel it no shame to have risen from such an origin; but I should feel it a shame to have sprung from one who prostituted the gifts of culture and eloquence to the service of prejudice and of falsehood."

Huxley was a tall, handsome man with sparkling dark eyes and a nose like a beak. First a surgeon, then a biologist, he made himself into a first-rate biblical scholar by intensive study. Darwin said of him: "His mind is as quick as a flash of lightning and as sharp as a razor." He seemed to take a special delight in pointing out that men of science were more moral than men of the cloth.

Although Huxley was known primarily as an agnostic rather than a humanist, he belonged in the humanist orbit. He once described moral purpose as "an article of exclusive human manufacture." Although he repudiated atheism as such, he declared that "there is no evidence of the existence of such a being as the god of the theologians." He even chided Herbert Spencer for spelling the word *Unknowable* with a capital letter, deploring this "ghost of an extinct philosophy." The following excerpts are taken from Huxley's 1889 essay "Agnosticism and Christianity,"

published in the 1898 Appleton book *Science and Christian Tradition.*
The writings of Cyril Bibby contain useful quotations and bibliographies.
—P.B.

Agnosticism Versus Christianity

The people who call themselves Agnostics have been charged
with doing so because they have not the courage to declare themselves Infidels. It has beem insinuated that they have adopted a
new name in order to escape the unpleasantness which attaches to
their proper denomination. . . . Agnosticism is not properly
described as a negative creed, nor indeed as a creed of any kind,
except insofar as it expressed absolute faith in the validity of a
principle, which is as much ethical as intellectual. This principle
may be stated in various ways but they all amount to this: that it is
wrong for a man to say that he is certain of the objective truth of
any proposition unless he can produce evidence which logically
justifies that certainty. This is what Agnosticism asserts; and in
my opinion it is all that is essential to Agnosticism. . . .

It was inevitable that a conflict should arise between Agnosticism and Theology; or rather, I ought to say, between Agnosticism and Ecclesiasticism. For Theology, the science, is one thing;
and Ecclesiasticism, the champion of a foregone conclusion as to
the truth of a particular form of Theology, is another. With scientific Theology, Agnosticism has no quarrel. . . .

But, as between Agnosticism and Eccelesiasticism, or, as our
neighbors across the Channel call it, Clericalism, there can be
neither peace nor truce. The Cleric asserts that it is morally wrong
not to believe certain propositions, whatever the results of a strict
scientific investigation of the evidence of these propositions. He
[Cardinal Newman] tells us "that religious error is, in itself, of an

immortal nature." He declares that he has prejudged certain conclusions, and looks upon those who show cause for arrest of judgment as emissaries of Satan. It necessarily follows that for him the attainment of faith, not the ascertainment of truth, is the highest aim of mental life. And on careful analysis of the nature of this faith, it will too often be found to be, not the mystic process of unity with the Divine, understood by the religious enthusiast, but that which the candid simplicity of a Sunday scholar once defined it to be. "Faith," said this unconscious plagiarist of Tertullian, "is the power of saying you believe things which are incredible."

Now I, and many other Agnostics, believe that faith in this sense is an abomination; and although we do not engage in the luxury of self-righteousness so far as to call those who are not of our way of thinking hard names, we do not feel that the disagreement between ourselves and those who hold this doctrine is even more moral than intellectual. . . .

The clerics and their lay allies commonly tell us that if we refuse to admit that there is good ground for expressing definite convictions about certain topics, the bonds of human society will dissolve and mankind lapse into savagery. There are several answers to this assertion. One is that the bonds of human society were formed without the aid of their theology; and in the opinion of not a few competent judges have been weakened rather than strengthened by a good deal of it. Greek science, Greek art, the ethics of old Israel, the social organization of old Rome, contrived to come into being without the help of anyone who believed in a single distinctive article of the simplest of the Christian creeds. The science, the art, the jurisprudence, the chief political and social theories of the modern world have grown out of those of Greece and Rome—not by favor of but in the teeth of the fundamental teachings of early Christianity, to which science, art, and any serious occupation with the things of this world were alike despicable. . . .

I think that even if the creeds from the so-called Apostles to the so-called Athanasian were swept into oblivion; and even if the human race should arrive at the conclusion that whether a bishop washes a cup or leaves it unwashed is not a matter of the least consequence, it will get on very well. The causes that have led to the development of morality in mankind, which guided or impelled us all the way from the savage to the civilized state, will not cease to operate because a number of ecclesiastical hypotheses turn out to be baseless. . . .

When Ecclesiasticism declares that we ought to believe this, that and the other, and are very wicked if we don't, it is impossible for us to give any answer but this: We have not the slightest objection to believe anything you like, if you will give good grounds for belief; but if you cannot, we must respectfully refuse, even if that refusal should wreck morality and insure our own damnation several times over. We are quite content to leave that to the decision of the future. The course of the past has impressed us with the firm conviction that no good ever comes of falsehood, and we feel warranted in refusing even to experiment in that direction.

Robert Ingersoll

Robert Green Ingersoll (1833-1899) was undoubtedly the most famous leader in the free thought movement in the United States during the nineteenth century. No other American ever did so much to make skepticism popular among common men. Although he was not a professional scholar, his influence also reached the religious and academic institutions of his time. Even the fundamentalists who railed at him, partially succumbed to his eloquence.

Although Ingersoll wrote forcefully—his collected works run to twelve volumes—literary production was not his forte. He excelled as a public lecturer in the days when lecturing was the favorite source of popular knowledge. His full-bellied oratory had no competition from television or loud speakers. His magic voice was rivalled only by that of William Jennings Bryan.

Ingersoll paid a fearful price for his campaign against Christian orthodoxy. In fact, he might have been elected president of the United States on the Republican ticket if he had not been branded as an "infidel."

Son of a rather foot-loose Congregational preacher, who happened to be a strong abolitionist, the young Robert arrived at an agnostic position slowly and painfully. For a time in his youth he attended an academy in an Illinois Baptist church. Being too poor to go directly to college, he tried his hand at rural school-teaching, then law. At the law his magnifent oratorical gifts soon brought him success.

When the Civil War came, Ingersoll organized a cavalry regiment and served successfully as its colonel. Entering politics, he became attorney general of Illinois and soon won national recognition as a political orator. His "plumed knight" speech for James G. Blaine at the Republican convention of 1876 became almost as famous as Bryan's later cross of gold speech—"[T]he people call for the man who has preserved in Congress what our soldiers won upon the field . . . for the man who has snatched the mask of democracy from the hideous face of rebellion. . . .

Like an armed warrior, like a plumed knight, James G. Blaine marched down the halls of the American Congress and threw his shining lance full and fair against the brazen foreheads of the defamers of his country and the maligners of his honor."

When Ingersoll began lecturing as a profession, he had many distinctly literary themes—Shakespeare was a favorite subject—but he found that his audiences preferred his all-out attacks on religion. So most of his lectures centered about the Bible, and ridicule became his major weapon. But he was often forced to avoid direct aspersions against orthodoxy because many states had antiblasphemy laws on their statute books, which made direct attacks on God and the Bible a crime.

Essentially, Ingersoll was a courageous humanist in the days when the word *humanist* was almost unknown. His own religion was summarized in the words, "to do all useful things, to reach with thought and deed the ideal in your brain . . . to look with trained and steady eyes for facts . . . to increase knowledge, to take burdens from the weak . . . to defend the right." His fundamentally hostile attitude toward orthodoxies was expressed in his lecture, *What Is Religion?* "Religion can never reform mankind because religion is slavery. It is far better to be free, to leave the forests and barricades of fear, to stand erect and face the future with a smile."

Here are three short samples of Ingersoll's style and content. His two best specialties were homely humor and blunt simplicity. The selection on the Trinity is from his lecture on *The Foundations of Faith*. The selection on "Questions for God" is from his last public address in 1899. The selection on "The Christian Heaven" is from *The Mistakes of Moses.*
—P.B.

The Trinity

Christ, according to the faith, is the second person of the Trinity, the Father being the first, and the Holy Ghost the third. Each of these three persons is God. Christ is his own father and his own son. The Holy Ghost is neither father nor son, but both. The son was begotten by the father, but existed before he was begotten—just the same before as after.

Christ is just as old as his father, and the father is just as young as his son. The Holy Ghost proceeded, from the Father and Son, but was equal to the Father and Son before he proceeded, that is to say, before he existed, but he is of the same age as the other two.

So it is declared that the Father is God and the Son God, and the Holy Ghost God, and that these three Gods make one God.

According to the celestial multiplication table, once one is three, and three times one is one, and according to heavenly subtraction if we take two from three, three are left. The addition is equally peculiar, if we add two to one we have but one. Each one is equal to himself and the other two. Nothing ever was, nothing ever can be more perfectly idiotic and absurd than the dogma of the Trinity.

Questions For God

It is asserted that an infinite God created all things, governs all things, and that the creature should be obedient and thankful to the creator; that the creator demands certain things, and that the person who complies with these demands is religious. . . .

For many centuries and by many people it was believed that this God demanded sacrifices; that he was pleased when parents shed the blood of their babes. Afterward it was supposed that he was satisfied with the blood of oxen, lambs, and doves, and that in exchange for or on account of these sacrifices, this God gave rain, sunshine, and harvest. It was also believed that if the sacrifices were not made, this God sent pestilence, famine, flood, and earthquake.

The last phase of this belief in sacrifice was, according to the

Christian doctrine, that God accepted the blood of his son, and that after his son had been murdered, he, God, was satisfied and wanted no more blood.

During all these years and by all these peoples it was believed that this God heard and answered prayer, that he forgave sins, and saved the souls of true believers. . . .

Now the questions are: Whether religion was founded on any known fact? Whether such a being as God exists? Whether he was the creator of yourself and myself? Whether any prayer was ever answered? Whether any sacrifice of babes or ox secured the favor of this unseen God? . . .

Why did he create the intellectually inferior?

Why did he create the deformed and helpless?

Why did he create the criminal, the idiotic, the insane?

Is he responsible for the centuries of slavery, for the backs that have been scarred with the lash, for the babes that have been sold from the breasts of mothers, for the families that have been separated and destroyed?

Is this God responsible for religious persecution, for the Inquisition, for the thumbscrew and rack, and for all the instruments of torture? . . .

What is such a God worth?

Would a decent man, having the power to prevent it, allow his enemies to torture and burn his friends? . . .

If a good and infinitely powerful God governs this world, how can we account for cyclones, earthquakes, pestilence, and famine?

How can we account for cancers, for microbes, for diphtheria, and the thousand diseases that prey on infancy? . . .

How can we account for a world where life feeds on life? Were beak and claw, tooth and fang, invented and produced by infinite mercy? . . .

Did infinite wisdom intentionally produce the beasts that feed upon the optic nerve? Think of blinding a man to satisfy the appetite of a microbe! Think of life feeding on life! Think of the victims! Think of the Niagara of blood pouring over the precipice of cruelty!

In view of these facts, what, after all, is religion? It is fear. Fear builds the altar and offers the sacrifice. Fear erects the, cathedral and bows the head of man in worship. Fear bends the knees and utters the prayer. Fear pretends to love. . . .

Lips, religious and fearful, tremblingly repeat this passage: "Though he slay me, yet will I trust him." This is the abyss of degradation.

The Christian Heaven

I want to give an idea or two in regard to the Christian heaven. Of all the selfish things in this world, it is one man wanting to get to heaven caring nothing what becomes of the rest of mankind. "If I can only get my little soul in." I have always noticed that the people who have the smallest souls make the most fuss about getting them saved.

Here is what we are taught by the Church today. We are taught by it that fathers and mothers, brothers and sisters, can all be happy in heaven, no matter what may be in hell; that the husband can be happy there with the wife that would have died for him at any moment of his life in hell. . . .

Here is a man seventy years of age who has been a splendid fellow and lived according the the laws of Nature. He has got about him splendid children whom he has loved and cared for with all his heart. But he did not happen to believe in the Bible; he did not believe in the Pentateuch; he did not believe that because some children made some fun of a gentleman who was short of hair, God sent two bears and tore the little darlings to pieces. He had a tender heart, and he thought about the mothers who would take the pieces, the bloody fragments of the children and press them to their bosoms in a frenzy of grief. He thought about their wails and lamentations and could not believe that God was such an infinite monster. That was all he thought, but he went to hell.

Then, there is another man who made a hell on earth for his wife, who had to be taken to an insane asylum, and his children were driven from home, and were wanderers and vagrants in the world. But just between the last sin and the last breath, this fellow got religion. He never did another thing except to take his medicine. He never did a solitary human being a favor, and he died and went to heaven.

Don't you think he would be astonished to see the other man in hell? And say to himself: "Is it possible that such a splendid character should bear fruit, and that all my rascality at last has brought me next to God?" . . .

Thomas Jefferson

It is now generally recognized that of all American statesmen who helped to shape the national policy on religious freedom, Thomas Jefferson comes first. Madison and Paine were very important but Jefferson was the most important. And it is very fortunate for all of us that the United States Supreme Court, in arriving at its decisions on church and state, has chosen Virginia, with Jefferson and Madison, rather than Massachusetts with its hide-bound Puritans as guides through church-state history.

Thomas Jefferson (1743-1826) has helped us to make this appraisal of his thinking about religion by directing that his own tombstone should read:

> Here was buried
> Thomas Jefferson
> Author of the Declaration of Independence
> Of the Statute of Virginia on Religious Freedom
> And Father of the University of Virginia
> Born April 1, 1743
> Died July 4, 1826

There is no mention on that tombstone of the fact that he was the third president of the United States.

Born into the Church of England, Jefferson in his youth came under some Calvinistic and Hugenot influence, in addition to the Anglican influence of his own home. This variety of faiths was important in molding the man. He tended, during the major part of his career, to avoid all sectarian controversy. In a letter written after his White House terms, he said that he had "never told my own religion, nor scrutinized that of another. I never attempted to make a convert, nor wished to change another's creed. I have ever judged of the religion of others by their lives. . . ."

One reason why he never "told [his] own religion" in his early years was that his views, when they occasionally leaked out, were branded as "infidel" by his political enemies. And this criticism extended even to his postpresidential years when some of his writings about religion were even banned in public libraries as being dangerous to American youth.

This was not surprising because Jefferson was a confessed Unitarian with an almost naive faith in the capacity of intellectual Unitarianism to conquer the masses by its sheer reasonableness. He should be described as a pro-Jesus Unitarian since he treasured a deep attachment to the Jesus of the New Testament, and he even issued a compilation of the sayings of Jesus in the New Testament and published the work under the title, *Life and Morals of Jesus*. It is not a very good book but it was a rather startling venture for a liberal layman.

Norman Cousins in his very interesting work, *In God We Trust*, quotes Jefferson's *Notes on Virginia* as follows:

> Difference of opinion is advantageous in religion. The several sects perform the office of a *censor morum* over each other. Is uniformity attainable? Millions of innocent men, women and children, since the introduction of Christianity, have been burnt, tortured, fined, imprisoned; yet we have not advanced one inch toward uniformity. What has been the effect of coercion? To make one half of the world fools and the other half hypocrites. To support roguery all over the earth. Let us reflect that it is inhabited by a thousand millions of people. That these profess probably a thousand different systems of religion. That ours is but one of that thousand.

This breadth of view in comparative religion was almost as shocking to orthodox Christians of Jefferson's day as outright atheism. And Jefferson confirmed some of their worst fears when his views became known. After retiring from the presidency he wrote to a friend: "My opinion is that there would never have been an infidel if there had never been a priest. The artificial structures they have built on the purest of all moral systems, for the purpose of deriving from it peace and power, revolt those who think for themselves."

I am quoting here the two most significant documents of Jefferson's religious career, his letter to the Connecticut Baptist Association of 1802, in which he coined the immortal phrase, "the wall of separation between church and state"; and an Act for Establishing Religious Freedom passed by the Assembly of Virginia in 1786 written by Jefferson. These two items of documentation have been taken with permission from Paul Kurtz's *American Thought Before 1900*, published by Macmillan.

—P.B.

Letter to the Danbury Baptists

Believing with you that religion is a matter which lies solely between man and his God, that he owes account to none other for his faith or his worship, that the legislative powers of government reach actions only, and not opinions, I contemplate with sovereign reverence that act of the whole American people which declared that their legislature should "make no law respecting an establishment of religion, or prohibiting the free exercise thereof," thus building a wall of separation between church and state. Adhering to this expression of the supreme will of the nation in behalf of the rights of conscience, I shall see with sincere satisfaction the progress of those sentiments which tend to restore to man all his natural rights, convinced he has no natural right in opposition to his social duties.

The Virginia Act For Establishing Religious Freedom

Well aware that Almighty God hath created the mind free; that all attempts to influence it by temporal punishments or burdens, or by civil incapacitations, tend only to beget habits of hypocrisy and meanness, and are a departure from the plan of the Holy Author of our religion, who being Lord both of body and mind, yet chose not to propagate it by coercions on either, as was in his Almighty power to do; that the impious presumption of legislators and rulers, civil as well as ecclesiastical, who, being themselves but fallible and uninspired men, have assumed dominion over the faith of others, setting up their own opinions and modes of thinking as the only true and infallible, and as such endeavoring to impose them on others, hath established and maintained false religions over the greatest part of the world, and through all time; that to compel a man to furnish contributions of money for the propagation of opinions which he disbelieves, is sinful and tyrannical; that even the forcing him to support this or that teacher of his own religious persuasion, is depriving him of the comfortable liberty of giving his contributions to the particular pastor whose morals he would make his pattern, and whose powers he feels most persuasive to righteousness, and is withdrawing from the ministry those temporal rewards, which, proceeding from an approbation of their personal conduct, are an additional incitement to earnest and unremitting labors for the instruction of mankind; that our civil rights have no dependence on our religious opinions, more than our opinions in physics or geometry; that, therefore, the proscribing any citizen as unworthy the public confidence by laying upon him an incapacity of being called to the offices of trust and emolument, unless he profess or renounce this or that religious opinion, is depriving him injuriously of those privileges and advantages to which in common with his fellow citizens he has a natural right; that it tends also to corrupt the principles of that very religion it is meant to encourage, by bribing, with a monopoly or worldly honors and emoluments, those who will externally profess and conform to it; that though indeed these are criminal who do not withstand such temptation, yet neither are those innocent who lay the bait in their way; that to suffer the civil magistrate to intrude his powers into the field of opinion and to restrain the profession or propagation of principles, on the supposition of their ill tendency, is a dangerous fallacy, which at once destroys all religious liberty, because he being of course judge of that tendency, will make his opinions the rule of judgment, and approve or condemn the sentiments of others only as they shall square with or differ from his

John F. Kennedy

Although John F. Kennedy, a committed Roman Catholic, cannot be classified as an official champion of free thought, he played an important role in the history of free thought in America by successfully challenging denominational bigotry. His address to the Greater Houston Ministerial Association on September 12, 1960 has become a classic document of religious tolerance. It was an honest and courageous speech, and it probably won him the presidency.

Kennedy adroitly defended his right to be a Catholic, and at the same time he undercut the power of his own church's bishops by accepting the Jeffersonian interpretation of the separation of church and state. He renounced tax support of parochial schools, the cherished dream of his bishops, and he even renounced the idea of appointing an American ambassador to the Vatican.

I had reminded him of the existence of Canon 1374 of his church's Canon Law, the canon that boycotts public schools for Catholic children by requiring that they get special permission from their bishops to attend such schools. He replied that he had not even heard of this canon until he was seventeen years old, when he was attending non-Catholic schools himself, and he specifically promised to oppose any such restriction on educational freedom.

He was true to this promise and, in fact, he was true to all the central promises made in his Houston speech. I can think of only one slight correction that needs to be made in that speech. Out of courtesy, no doubt, he praised the Catholic bishops for an ambiguous 1948 statement in which they allegedly "endorsed church-state separation." Their endorsement was ecclesiastical doubletalk, since they continued fiercely to demand tax dollars for their enterprises and to denounce the Supreme Court for eliminating religious instruction in public schools.

The text of Kennedy's Houston speech was carried in several national newspapers on September 13, 1960, and in Patricia Barrett's scholarly *Religious Liberty and the American Presidency.*

—P.B.

97

Kennedy's Houston Speech

I am grateful for your generous invitation to state my views. While the so-called religious issue is necessarily and properly the chief topic here tonight, I want to emphasize from the outset that we have far more critical issues to face in the 1960 election: The spread of Communist influence, until it now festers ninety miles off the coast of Florida—the humiliating treatment of our president and vice president by those who no longer respect our power —the hungry children I saw in West Virginia, the old people who cannot pay their doctor bills, the families forced to give up their farms—an America with too many slums, with too few schools, and too late to the moon and outer space.

These are the real issues which should decide this campaign. And they are not religious issues—for war and hunger and ignorance and despair know no religious barriers.

But because I am a Catholic, and no Catholic has ever been elected president, the real issues in this campaign have been obscured—perhaps deliberately, in some quarters less responsible than this. So it is apparently necessary for me to state once again—not what kind of church I believe in, for that should be important only to me—but what kind of America I believe in.

I believe in an America where the separation of church and state is absolute—where no Catholic prelate would tell the president (should he be Catholic) how to act, and no Protestant minister would tell his parishioners for whom to vote—where no church or church school is granted any public funds or political preference—and where no man is denied public office merely because his religion differs from the president who might appoint him or the people who might elect him.

I believe in an America that is officially neither Catholic, Protestant nor Jewish—where no public official either requests or accepts instructions on public policy from the pope, the National Council of Churches or any other ecclesiastical source—where no religious body seeks to impose its will directly or indirectly upon the general populace or the public acts of its officials—and where religious liberty is so indivisible that an act against one church is treated as an act against all.

For, while this year it may be a Catholic against whom the finger of suspicion is pointed, in other years it has been, and may someday be again, a Jew—or a Quaker—or a Unitarian—or a Baptist. It was Virginia's harassment of Baptist preachers, for example, that helped lead to Jefferson's statute of religious freedom. Today I may be the victim—but tomorrow it may be you—until the whole fabric of our harmonious society is ripped at a time of great national peril.

Finally, I believe in an America where religious intolerance will someday end—where all men and all churches are treated as equals—where every man has the same right to attend or not attend the church of his choice—where there is no Catholic vote, no anti-Catholic vote, no bloc voting of any kind—and where Catholics, Protestants and Jews, at both the lay and pastoral level, will refrain from those attitudes of disdain and division which have so often marred their works in the past, and promote instead the American ideal of brotherhood.

That is the kind of America in which I believe, and it represents the kind of presidency in which I believe—a great office that must neither be humbled by making it the instrument of any one religious group, nor tarnished by arbitrarily withholding its occupancy from the members of any one religious group. I believe in a president whose religious views are his own private affair, neither imposed by him upon the nation nor imposed by the nation upon him as a condition to holding that office.

I would not look with favor upon a president working to subvert the First Amendment's guarantees of religious liberty. Nor would our system of checks and balances permit him to do so—and neither do I look with favor upon those who would work to subvert Article VI of the Constitution by requiring a religious test—even by indirection—for it. If they disagree with that safeguard, they should be out openly working to repeal it.

I want a chief executive whose public acts are responsible to all groups and obligated to none—who can attend any ceremony, service or dinner his office may appropriately require of him—and whose fulfillment of his presidential oath is not limited or conditioned by any religious oath, ritual or obligation.

This is the kind of America I believe in—and this is the kind I fought for in the South Pacific and the kind my brother died for in Europe. No one suggested then that we might have a "divided loyalty," that we did "not believe in liberty" or that we belonged to a disloyal group that threatened the "freedoms for which our forefathers died."

And in fact this is the kind of America for which our forefathers died—when they fled here to escape religious test oaths that denied office to members of less favored churches—when they fought for the Constitution, the Bill of Rights, and the Virginia Statute of Religious Freedom—and when they fought at the shrine I visited today, the Alamo. For side by side with Bowie and Crockett died McCafferty and Bailey and Carey—but no one knows whether they were Catholics or not. For there was no religious test at the Alamo.

I ask you tonight to follow in that tradition—to judge me on the basis of my record of fourteen years in Congress—on my declared stands against an ambassador to the Vatican, against unconstitutional aid to parochial schools, and against any boycott of the public schools (which I have attended myself)—instead of judging me on the basis of these pamphlets and publications we all have seen that carefully select quotations out of context from the statements of Catholic church leaders, usually in other countries, frequently in other centuries and rarely relevant to any situation here—and always omitting, of course, the statement of the American Bishops in 1948 which strongly endorsed church-state separation, and which more nearly reflects the views of almost every American Catholic. I do not consider these other quotations binding upon my public acts—why should you? But let me say with respect to other countries, that I am wholly opposed to the state being used by any religious group, Catholic or Protestant, to compel, prohibit or persecute the free exercise of any other religion. And I hope that you and I condemn with equal fervor those nations which deny their presidency to Protestants and those which deny it to Catholics. And rather than cite the misdeeds of those who differ, I would cite the record of the Catholic Church in such nations as Ireland and France—and the independence of such statesmen as Adenauer and De Gaulle.

But let me stress again that these are my views—for, contrary to common newspaper usage, I am not the Catholic candidate for president. I am the Democratic party's candidate for president, who happens also to be a Catholic. I do not speak for my church on public matters—and the church does not speak for me.

Whatever issue may come before me as president—on birth control, divorce, censorship, gambling, or any other subject—I will make my decision in accordance with these views, in accordance with what my conscience tells me to be the national interest, and without regard to outside religious pressures or dictates. And no power or threat of punishment could cause me to decide otherwise.

But if the time should ever come—and I do not concede any conflict to be even remotely possible—when my office would require me to either violate my conscience or violate the national interest, then I would resign the office; and I hope any conscientious public servant would do the same.

But I do not intend to apologize for these views to my critics of either Catholic or Protestant faith—nor do I intend to disavow either my views or my church in order to win this election. If I should lose on the real issues, I shall return to my seat in the Senate, satisfied that I had tried my best and was fairly judged. But if this election is decided on the basis that forty million Americans lost their chance of being president on the day they were baptized, then it is the whole nation that will be the loser, in the eyes of Catholics and non-Catholics around the world, in the eyes of history, and in the eyes of our own people.

But if, on the other hand, I should win the election, then I shall devote every effort of mind and spirit to fulfilling the oath of the presidency—practically identical, I might add, to the oath I have taken for fourteen years in the Congress. For, without reser-

W. E. H. Lecky

William Edward Hartpole Lecky (1838-1903) was one of the first great historians of ideas, a free-lance writer who influenced the whole course of European and American culture although he never served as a university professor. In the free thought movement of the nineteenth century his two great works on rationalism and morals stand out as models, *History of the Rise and Influence of the Spirit of Rationalism in Europe* (hereafter called *Rationalism*) and *History of European Morals*.

One key to his success was money. He came from a landlord family of Scotch origin that owned land near Dublin, and his family income made it possible to devote his whole life to research and writing. Never was money spent more fruitfully. He wandered freely and expensively over nearly all of Europe, probing into those sensitive, cultural areas which other historians were reluctant to write about. He learned to read easily in Greek, Latin, German, Italian, Spanish and French. His *Rationalism* was produced when he was only twenty-seven and his European morals work before he was thirty. *Rationalism* was a run-away bestseller, being reprinted more than twenty times in its first fifty years.

Although Lecky declined a chair at Oxford, he did decide to run as a Liberal-Unionist candidate for the British Parliament. He was elected and served for about ten years, but he was rather unhappy in the House because he found that politics interfered with his writing.

Lecky was not an all-out enemy of Christianity, but the total effect of his writing was clearly anti-orthodox. He specialized in exposing the worst results of ecclesiastical ignorance and tyranny. He was equally frank in discussing the shortcomings of Protestantism and Catholicism. For him Luther seemed almost as unacceptable as a pope. The two great devils in his discourses were intolerance and terror. Who could forget his description of the torture of witches?

> If the witch was obdurate, the first, and it was said the most effectual method of obtaining confession was by what was termed "waking her." An

iron bridle or hoop was bound across her face with four prongs which were thrust into her mouth. It was fastened behind to the wall by a chain, in such a manner that the victim was unable to lie down; and in this position she was sometimes kept for several days, while men were constantly with her to prevent her from closing her eyes for a moment of sleep . . . long pins were thrust into her body . . . excessive thirst was often added to her tortures. . . .

I have chosen to reproduce here two passages from Lecky's *Rationalism*, the first concerning the "unblushing mendacity" of the ages of faith, and the second concerning the horrors of witchcraft and magic. One sociological footnote used by Lecky in discussing witchcraft and persecution is worth recording. "The overwhelming majority of witches," he said, "were extremely poor."

—P.B.

Unblushing Mendacity

The Fathers laid down as a distinct proposition that pious frauds were justifiable and even laudable; and if they had not laid this down, they would nevertheless have practised them as a necessary consequence of their doctrine of exclusive salvation. Immediately all ecclesiastical literature became tainted with a spirit of the most unblushing mendacity. Heathenism was to be combated, and therefore prophecies of Christ by Orpheus and the Sibyls were forged, lying wonders were multiplied, and ceaseless calumnies poured upon those who, like Julian, opposed the faith. Heretics were to be convinced, and therefore interpolations of old writings or complete forgeries were habitually opposed to the forged Gospels. The veneration of relics and the monastic system were introduced, and therefore innumerable miracles were attributed to the bones of saints or to the prayers of hermits, and were solemnly asserted by the most eminent of the Fathers.

The tendency was not confined to those Eastern nations which had been always almost destitute of the sense of truth; it triumphed wherever the supreme importance of dogmas was held. Generation after generation it became more universal; it continued till the very sense of truth and the very love of truth seemed blotted out from the minds of men.

That this is no exaggerated picture of the condition at which the middle ages arrived, is known to all who have any acquaintance with its literature; for during that gloomy period the only scholars in Europe were priests and monks, who conscientiously believed that no amount of falsehood was reprehensible which conduced to the edification of the people. Not only did they pursue with the grossest calumny every enemy to their faith, not only did they encircle every saint with a halo of palpable fiction, not only did they invent tens of thousands of miracles for the purpose of stimulating devotion—they also very naturally carried into all other subjects the indifference to truth they had acquired in theology. All their writings, and more especially their histories, became tissues of the wildest fables, so grotesque and at the same time so audacious, that they were the wonder of succeeding ages.

And the very men who scattered these fictions broadcast over Christendom, taught at the same time that credulity was a virtue and skepticism a crime. As long as the doctrine of exclusive salvation was believed and realized, it was necessary for the peace of mankind that they should be absolutely certain of the truth of what they believed; in order to be so certain, it was necessary to suppress adverse arguments; and in order to effect this object, it was necessary that there should be no critical or skeptical spirit in Europe. A habit of boundless credulity was therefore a natural consequence of the doctrine of exclusive salvation; and not only did this habit necessarily produce a luxuriant crop of falsehood, it was itself the negation of the spirit of truth.

The Horrors of Witchcraft

I propose in the present chapter to examine that vast department of miracles, which is comprised under the several names of
witchcraft, magic, and sorcery. It is a subject which has, I think,
scarcely obtained the position it deserves in the history of opinions, having been too generally treated in the spirit of the anti-
quarian, as if it belonged entirely to the past, and could have no
voice or bearing upon the controversies of the present. Yet, for
more than fifteen hundred years, it was universally believed that
the Bible established, in the clearest manner, the reality of the
crime, and that an amount of evidence, so varied and so ample as
to preclude the very possibility of doubt, attested its continuance
and its prevalence.

The clergy denounced it with all the emphasis of authority.
The legislators of almost every land enacted laws for its punishment. Acute judges, whose lives were spent in sifting evidence,
investigated the question on countless occasions, and condemned
the accused. Tens of thousands of victims perished by the most
agonising and protracted torments, without exciting the faintest
compassion; and, as they were for the most part extremely
ignorant and extremely poor, sectarianism and avarice had but
little influence on the subject.

Nations that were completely separated by position, by interests, and by character, on this one question were united. In almost
every province of Germany, but especially in those where clerical
influence predominated, the persecution raged with a fearful
intensity. Seven thousand victims are said to have been burned at
Trèves, six hundred by a single bishop of Bamberg, and eight
hundred in a single year in the bishopric of Würtzburg.

In France, decrees were passed on the subject by the Parliaments of Paris, Toulouse, Bordeaux, Rheimes, Rouen, Dijon, and Rennes, and they were all followed by a harvest of blood. At Toulouse, the seat of the Inquisition, four hundred persons perished for sorcery at a single execution, and fifty at Douay in a single year. Remy, a judge of Nancy, boasted that he had put to death eight hundred witches in sixteen years. The executions that took place at Paris in a few months were, in the emphatic words of an old writer, "almost infinite."

The fugitives who escaped to Spain were there seized and burned by the Inquisition. In that country the persecution spread to the smallest towns, and the belief was so deeply rooted in the popular mind, that a sorcerer was burnt as late as 1780. Torquemada devoted himself to the extirpation of witchcraft as zealously as to the extirpation of heresy, and he wrote a book upon the enormity of the crime. In Italy, a thousand persons were executed in a single year in the province of Como; and in other parts of the country, the severity of the inquisitors at last created an absolute rebellion. The same scenes were enacted in the wild valleys of Switzerland and of Savoy. In Geneva, which was then ruled by a bishop, five hundred alleged witches were executed in three months; forty-eight were burnt at Constance or Ravensburg, and eighty in the little town of Valery, in Savoy. In 1670, seventy persons were condemned in Sweden, and a large proportion of them were burnt. And these are only a few of the more salient events in that long series of persecutions which extended over almost every country, and continued for centuries with unabated fury.

The Church of Rome proclaimed in every way that was in her power the reality and the continued existence of the crime. She strained every nerve to stimulate the persecution. She taught by all her organs that to spare a witch was a direct insult to the Almighty, and to her ceaseless exertions is to be attributed by far the greater proportion of the blood that was shed. In 1484, Pope Innocent VIII. issued a bull which gave a fearful impetus to the persecution, and he it was who commissioned the Inquisitor Sprenger, whose book was long the recognised manual on the subject, and who is said to have condemned hundreds to death every year. Similar bulls were issued by Julius II. in 1504, and by Adrian VI. in 1523. A long series of Provincial Councils asserted the existence of sorcery, and anathematised those who resorted to it. "The universal practice of the Church was to place magic and sorcery among the reserved cases, and at prônes to declare magicians and sorcerers excommunicated"; and a form of exorcism was solemnly inserted in the ritual.

Almost all the great works that were written in favour of the executions were written by ecclesiastics. Almost all the lay works on the same side were dedicated to and sanctioned by ecclesiastical dignitaries. Ecclesiastical tribunals condemned thousands to death, and countless bishops exerted all their influence to multiply the victims. In a word, for many centuries it was universally believed, that the continued existence of witchcraft formed an integral part of the teaching of the Church, and that the persecution that raged through Europe was supported by the whole stress of her infallibility.

Such was the attitude of the Church of Rome with reference to this subject, but on this ground the Reformers had no conflict with their opponents. The credulity which Luther manifested on all matters connected with diabolical intervention, was amazing, even for his age; and, when speaking of witchcraft, his language was emphatic and unhesitating. "I would have no compassion on these witches," he exclaimed, "I would burn them all!"

James Madison

James Madison (1751-1836), fourth president of the United States, has been promoted by historians to the first rank among defenders of American religious freedom. He was the leader of the movement for our Bill of Rights and is therefore entitled to be called author of the First Amendment. He wrote the "Memorial and Remonstrance Against Religious Assessments" of 1785 which won the battle against tax support in Virginia; and he constantly expressed throughout his life those Constitutional principles of religious freedom and church-state separation which have formed the foundation of American policy.

One reason for Madison's eminence in this field was that he studied religion carefully. In his youth he started on the road to the Anglican pulpit, and then changed his mind. One factor in bringing about the change was that he became disgusted with the narrowmindedness of the clergy. In public statements and letters—see Saul Padover's *The Complete Madison*—he scored both preachers and priests for religious persecution. As a young man he wrote: "That diabolical, hell-conceived principle of persecution rages among some; and to their eternal infamy, the clergy can furnish their quota of imps for such business." In his early years Madison was horrified when his home colony of Virginia jailed six Baptist preachers "for publishing religious sentiments which in the main are very orthodox."

He insisted on religious equality for Jews and also for Roman Catholics, although his unflattering opinion of the Roman hierarchy has been recorded in a famous statement: "In the Papal System, Government and Religion are in a manner consolidated, and that is found to be the worst of Governments." In a letter of 1822 to Edward Livingston, he said: "We are teaching the world the great truth that governments do better without Kings and Nobles than with them. The merit will be doubled by the other lesson that Religion flourishes in greater purity without than with the aid of Government."

Madison carried his opposition to tax support for religion to the point where he opposed paid chaplains in both the armed services and in Congress. "Look through the armies and navies of the world," he said, "and say whether the appointment of their ministers of religion, the spiritual interest of the flocks or the temporal interest of the shepherds, be most in view." As to paid chaplains in Congress, he declared that the whole scheme of purchased prayer and paid clergymen "is a palpable violation of equal rights, as well as of Constitutional principles. The tenets of the chaplains elected (by the majority) shut the door of worship against the members whose creeds and consciences forbid a participation in that of the majority."

I am inserting here major parts of the text of Madison's "Memorial and Remonstrance" as reprinted officially by the Supreme Court in the text of the Everson bus case in 1947. It is one of the most important documents in the history of our law. It is not, of course, a free-thought document except by inference. Madison was scarcely a freethinker. He was cooly theistic, cautiously orthodox when the situation demanded it. He interlarded his expressions of religious neutrality with the clichés of orthodox. Nominally he put "homage to the Creator" ahead of "the claims of Civil Society." But no American in our history has done more for the financial separation of church and state.

—P.B.

Memorial and Remonstrance Against Religious Assessments

TO THE HONORABLE THE GENERAL ASSEMBLY
OF THE COMMONWEALTH OF VIRGINIA.
A MEMORIAL AND REMONSTRANCE.

We, the subscribers, citizens of the said Commonwealth, having taken into serious consideration, a Bill printed by order of the last Session of General Assembly, entitled "A Bill establishing a provision for Teachers of the Christian Religion," and conceiving that the same, if finally armed with the sanctions of a law, will be a dangerous abuse of power, are bound as faithful members of a free State, to remonstrate against it, and to declare the reasons by which we are determined. We remonstrate against the said Bill.

1. Because we hold it for a fundamental and undeniable truth, "that Religion or the duty which we owe to our Creator and the Manner of discharging it, can be directed only by reason and conviction, not by force or violence."

The Religion then of every man must be left to the conviction and conscience of every man; and it is the right of every man to exercise it as these may dictate. This right is in its nature an unalienable right. It is unalienable; because the opinions of men, depending only on the evidence contemplated by their own minds, cannot follow the dictates of other men: It is unalienable also; because what is here a right towards men, is a duty towards the Creator. It is the duty of every man to render to the Creator such homage, and such only, as he believes to be acceptable to him. This duty is precedent both in order of time and degree of obligation, to the claims of Civil Society. Before any man can be considered as a member of Civil Society, he must be considered as a subject of the Governor of the Universe: And if a member of Civil Society, who enters into any subordinate Association, must always do it with a reservation of his duty to the general authority; much more must every man who becomes a member of any particular Civil Society, do it with a saving of his allegiance to the Universal Sovereign. We maintain therefore that in matters of Religion, no man's right is abridged by the institution of Civil Society, and that Religion is wholly exempt from its cognizance. True it is, that no other rule exists, by which any question which may divide a Society, can be ultimately determined, but the will of the majority; but it is also true, that the majority may trespass on the rights of the minority.

2. Because if religion be exempt from the authority of the Society at large, still less can it be subject to that of the Legislative Body. The latter are but the creatures and vicegerents of the former. Their jurisdiction is both derivative and limited: it is limited with regard to the coordinate departments, more necessarily is it limited with regard to the constituents.

The preservation of a free government requires not merely,

that the metes and bounds which separate each department of power may be invariably maintained; but more especially, that neither of them be suffered to overleap the great Barrier which defends the rights of the people. The Rulers who are guilty of such an encroachment, exceed the commission from which they derive their authority, and are Tyrants. The People who submit to it are governed by laws made neither by themselves, nor by an authority derived from them, and are slaves.

3. Because, it is proper to take alarm at the first experiment on our liberties. We hold this prudent jealousy to be the first duty of citizens, and one of [the] noblest characteristics of the late Revolution. The freeman of America did not wait till usurped power had strengthened itself by exercise, and entangled the question in precedents. They saw all the consequences in the principle, and they avoided the consequences by denying the principle. We revere this lesson too much, soon to forget it. Who does not see that the same authority which can establish Christianity, in exclusion of all other Religions, may establish with the same ease any particular sect of Christians, in exclusion of all other Sects? That the same authority which can force a citizen to contribute three pence only of his property for the support of any one establishment, may force him to conform to any other establishment in all cases whatsoever?

4. Because, the bill violates that equality which ought to be the basis of every law, and which is more indispensible, in proportion as the validity or expediency of any law is more liable to be impeached. If "all men are by nature equally free and independent," all men are to be considered as entering into Society on equal conditions; as relinquishing no more, and therefore retaining no less, one than another, of their natural rights. Above all are they to be considered as retaining an "*equal* title to the free exercise of Religion according to the dictates of conscience."

Whilst we assert for ourselves a freedom to embrace, to profess and to observe the Religion which we believe to be of divine origin, we cannot deny an equal freedom to those whose minds have not yet yielded to the evidence which has convinced us. If this freedom be abused, it is an offence against God, not against man: To God, therefore, not to men, must an account of it be rendered. As the Bill violates equality by subjecting some to peculiar burdens; so it violates the same principle, by granting to others peculiar exemptions. Are the Quakers and Menonists the only sects who think a compulsive support of their religions unnecessary and unwarrantable? Can their piety alone be intrusted with the care of public worship? Ought their Religions to be endowed above all others, with extraordinary privileges, by which proselytes may be enticed from all others? We think, too favorably of the justice and good sense of these denominations, to believe that they either covet preeminencies over their fellow citizens, or that they will be seduced by them, from the common opposition to the measure.

5. Because the bill implies either that the Civil Magistrate is a competent Judge of Religious truth; or that he may employ Religion as an engine of Civil policy. The first is an arrogant pretension falsified by the contradictory opinions of Rulers in all ages, and throughout the world: The second an unhallowed perversion of the means of salvation. . . .

7. Because experience witnesseth that ecclesiastical establishments, instead of maintaining the purity and efficacy of Religion, have had a contrary operation. During almost fifteen centuries, has the legal establishment of Christianity been on trial. What have been its fruits? More or less in all places, pride and indolence in the Clergy; ignorance and servility in the laity; in both, superstition, bigotry, and persecution. . . .

8. Because the establishment in question is not necessary for the support of Civil Government. If it be urged as necessary for the support of Civil Government only as it is a means of supporting Religion, and it be not necessary for the latter purpose, it cannot be necessary for the former. If Religion be not within [the] cognizance of Civil Government, how can its legal establishment be said to be necessary to civil Government? What influence in fact have ecclesiastical establishments had on Civil Society? In some instances they have been seen to erect a spiritual tyranny on the ruins of Civil authority; in many instances they have been seen upholding the thrones of political tyranny; in no instance have they been seen the guardians of the liberties of the people.

Rulers who wished to subvert the public liberty, may have

found an established clergy convenient auxiliaries. A just government, instituted to secure and perpetuate it, needs them not. Such
a government will be best supported by protecting every citizen in
the enjoyment of his Religion with the same equal hand which
protects his person and his property; by neither invading the
equal rights of any Sect, nor suffering any Sect to invade those of
another. . . .

11. Because, it will destroy the moderation and harmony
which the forbearance of our laws to intermeddle with Religion,
has produced amongst its several sects. Torrents of blood have
been split in the old world, by vain attempts of the secular arm to
extinguish Religious discord, by proscribing all difference in
Religious opinions. Time has at length revealed the true remedy.
Every relaxation of narrow and rigorous policy, wherever it has
been tried, has been found to assuage the disease. The American
Theatre has exhibited proofs, that equal and compleat liberty, if
it does not wholly eradicate it, sufficiently destroys its malignant
influence on the health and prosperity of the State. If with the
salutary effects of this system under our own eyes, we begin to
contract the bonds of Religious freedom, we know no name that
will too severely reproach our folly. At least let warning be taken
at the first fruits of the threatened innovation. The very appearance of the Bill has transformed that Christian forbearance, love
and charity, which of late mutually prevailed, into animosities
and jealousies, which may not soon be appeased. What mischiefs
may not be dreaded should this enemy to the public quiet be
armed with the force of a law? . . .

13. Because attempts to enforce by legal sanctions, acts
obnoxious to so great a proportion of Citizens, tend to enervate
the laws in general, and to slacken the bands of Society. If it be
difficult to execute any law which is not generally deemed necessary or salutary, what must be the case where it is deemed invalid
and dangerous? and what may be the effect of so striking an
example of impotency in the Government, on its general authority.

Joseph McCabe

Probably the most prolific writer in the whole history of free thought was the English ex-priest, Joseph McCabe. He wrote more than three hundred books and delivered at least three thousand lectures. Before he died in his eighties, he had become known as the most scholarly—and also the most quarrelsome—rationalist in the world. He even quarreled with his old sponsors, the British Rationalist Press Association, but he became reconciled to the RPA before his death.

Born in Lancashire in 1867, McCabe came from a poverty-stricken conservative home where Roman Catholicism prevailed. He began training for the priesthood at the age of fifteen, was ordained at twenty-three and soon became a Franciscan monk and a professor of philosophy in a Catholic college. He demonstrated exceptional gifts in mastering Greek, Latin, Hebrew, French, and German.

His inquisitive mind soon made him a skeptic. He drew up a list of the arguments for and against belief in the existence of God and immortality, wrote *bankrupt* at the bottom of the list, and walked out of the monastery at the age of twenty-eight.

His first famous book was *Twelve Years in a Monastery*, an account of his own experience. On the strength of that success he became a popular lecturer, branching out into the whole world of modern culture and translating works from five languages. Coming to America, he was received with open arms by the Kansas publisher, E. Haldeman-Julius, who persuaded him to write at least fifty Little Blue Books, which sold by the millions. He is alleged to have written these Little Blue Books at the rate of one a week.

McCabe wrote with great power in exposing the evils of the monasticism which had nearly ruined his own life. He declared that "the monastic system is a fraud and hypocrisy from beginning to end. . . . [A]bout one monk in ten is deeply religious, and about one in ten quite unscrupulous . . . about half are immoral . . . seven or eight in ten have no such religious sentiment as their profession demands, and their life would be intolerable but for the generous supply of liquor, the almost complete neglect (in the house) of their regulations, the possession by each of money (in defiance of their vows), and the incessant visiting of their lady parishioners. Their long religious ceremonies are an empty and a dreary formalism. Their life is, in spirit and letter, one sustained defiance of their professions."

I regard McCabe as an overly-vehement prophet, but I respect him profoundly for his courage and his scholarship. In his closing years he became frightfully anti-American, but who is to say that American foreign policy did not earn his condemnation?

With the kind consent of the heirs of Haldeman-Julius, I have chosen several passages from McCabe's most gigantic tome, *The Story of Religious Controversy*, published by the Stratford Company of Boston in 1929, with an introduction by Haldeman-Julius.

—P.B.

The Masquerade of Creeds

If it were a question of a single point, evolution, as Fundamentalists generally imagine, it is just conceivable that a man might for a time suspend his judgment, but the situation is very different from this. While eight sets of experts prove evolution, another set prove by its internal evidence that the Pentateuch was not written until about 500 B.C.; another set derive from the ruins of Babylonia and Assyria legends of creation, Eden, fall, and deluge identity; another set show that the history of the race has deluge so closely corresponding to the Hebrew legends that no one can doubt their identity; another set show that the history of the race has been quite different from the story of the Old Testament. And so on.

Against this mass of evidence accumulated by independent bodies of the most highly trained students in the world, the Fundamentalist can only put . . . what? In ninety-nine cases out of a hundred he could not even tell you why he believes the Old

Testament to be "the Word of God." . . .

Therefore, the position, not merely of the Fundamentalist and the Roman Catholic, but of any Christian who holds the doctrines of the creation and fall of man, and the miraculous birth, atoning death, and resurrection of Christ, is quite plain. He is in flat and flagrant conflict with science. . . .

I am not concerned here with believers who put new interpretations on the old doctrines of creation, original sin, atonement, resurrection, and so forth. I share the scorn of the Fundamentalist for such things. They mean, in plain American, that the Christian doctrines have been abandoned.

In one of my works (*The Religion of Sir Oliver Lodge,* 1914) I analyzed the various professions of faith of a British scientist who, while holding spiritualistic views, declares himself a member of the Church of England. . . . And this is how, from the study of his works, I find him accepting the simplest of the creeds:

> I believe in God—a God who is one with Nature,
> The Father Almighty—but not all-powerful,
> Creator of Heaven and Earth—which were not created, but are eternal,
> And in Jesus Christ, His only son, our Lord—who is, however, a son of God only in the same sense as we, but more so,
> Who was conceived by the Holy Ghost—as an artist conceives his work, not miraculously,
> Born of the Virgin Mary—who was not a virgin,
> Suffered under Pontius Pilate, was crucified, dead and buried— not to atone for the sins of the world,
> The third day he rose again from the dead—or his soul made a new body out of ether,
> He ascended into heaven—or made a final phantasmal appearance,
> Sitteth on the right hand (which doesn't exist) of God the Father Almighty (who is not Almighty)—though there is no heaven to sit in,
> From thence he shall come to judge the living and the dead—that is to say, he will persuade them to judge themselves,
> I believe in the Holy Ghost—which is a figure of speech,
> The Holy Catholic Church—certainly not the Roman, and the Anglo-Catholic only as it imposes no belief on me,
> The communion of saints—by telepathy,
> The forgiveness of sins—each man forgiving himself,

> The resurrection of the body—which certainly won't rise again,
> And life everlasting—which may not last forever; we don't know.

I understand that Sir Oliver Lodge was a little peeved when my very careful reconstruction of his creed appeared. But it is strictly based upon his works. . . . It is the creed of the extreme modernists, and on some such line runs the creed of all who no longer accept such doctrines as hell, heaven, atonement, and so on. All that we need say here is that they are Christians who believe that Paul and the Christian Church have been wrong in nearly everything until science began to enlighten the world.

With the Fundamentalists the conflict is to the death; and one needs no gift of prophecy to say which combatant will die. The plea of Fundamentalist leaders that they are not opposed to true science is too transparent an imposture to deceive their followers long. "True science" obviously means the science which does not conflict with their medieval views.

H. L. Mencken

That veteran curmudgeon, Henry Lewis Mencken (1880-1956) has been described as "the first man in our literature to raise invective to the level of art."

From the free thought point of view Mencken deserves all the accolades that can be heaped upon him. In the area of religion he was a fearless critic and a responsible biblical scholar. I would rank his *Treatise on the Gods* as the most effective exposé of organized religion ever written by an American, and many of his other works in the field of religious criticism—such as his *Treatise on Right and Wrong* and his *Prejudices* series—are close to it in quality. In attacking democracy he often indulged in reckless vituperation; in attacking religion he retained the vituperation but revealed real scholarship.

He took particular delight in attacking fundamentalist Protestantism which he called "the more homicidal variety of wowserism." This was partly because Protestantism during his heyday was coupled with that phenomenon which he considered social insanity, Prohibition. His attack on Catholicism was devastating but much more brief, and it was tinctured with some slight admiration "despite its frequent astounding imbecilities." "The truth is," he said, "that the Catholic system is in its very essence inimical to intelligence, and commonly either throttles it or drives it out of the fold." "Theoretically," he said, "the Pope could declare cannibalism lawful tomorrow, and even exact it as a duty, and there would be no way for his mandate to be upset, save maybe by the lame process of finding him insane."

Mencken's attack on Christianity went to the heart of the gospel. "Faith," he said, "may be defined briefly as an illogical belief in the occurrence of the improbable." His scorn of orthodoxy extended to the whole American system of higher education, which he rejected for himself in favor of a difficult personal career in daily journalism. In Baltimore and New York he showed astonishing journalistic gifts, and when he launched his own magazine—the *American Mercury* after the *Smart*

Set—he became, for a time, America's leading literary critic.

On Theologians

The truth is that Christian theology, like every other theology, is not only opposed to the scientific spirit; it is also opposed to all other attempts at rational thinking. Not by accident does Genesis 3 make the father of knowledge a serpent—slimy, sneaking and abominable. Since the earliest days the church as an organization has thrown itself violently against every effort to liberate the body and mind of man. It has been, at all times and everywhere, the habitual and incorrigible defender of bad governments, bad laws, bad social theories, bad institutions. It was, for centuries, an apologist for slavery, as it was the apologist for the divine right of kings.

The English bishops voted almost unanimously against every proposal to liberate the laws of the empire, and the popes opposed every effort to establish freedom of thought in free states. In the domain of pure ideas one branch of the church clings to the archaic speculations of Thomas Aquinas and the other labors under the preposterous nonsense of John Calvin. . . .

The notion that science does not concern itself with first causes—that it leaves that field to theology or metaphysics, and confines itself to mere effects—this notion has no support in the plain facts. If it could, science would explain the origin of life on earth at once—and there is every reason to believe that it will do so on some not too remote tomorrow. To argue that the gaps in knowledge which will confront the seeker must be filled, not by patient inquiry, but by intuition or revelation, is simply to give ignorance a gratuitous and preposterous dignity. . . .

The evidence of the emotions, save in cases where it has strong objective support, is really no evidence at all, for every recognizable emotion has its opposite, and if one points one way then another points the other way. Thus the familiar argument that there is an instinctive desire for immortality, and that this desire proves it to be a fact, becomes puerile when it is recalled that there is also a powerful and widespread fear of annihilation, and that this fear, on the same principle proves that there is nothing beyond the grave. Such childish "proofs" are typically theological, and they remain theological even when they are adduced by men who like to flatter themselves by believing that they are scientific gents. . . .

It is the custom of the reconcilers of science and religion to seek a miserable peace with the theologians by putting an arbitrary limit upon this increase in human knowledge. Eager to pass as virtuous, they give assurances that science will stop before it gets into really close quarters with divinity. Some of them even go to the length of hinting that some of the laws already established are probably dubious, and must be subordinated to theological dogma. But this is politics, not sense.

There is, in fact, no reason to believe that any given natural phenomenon, however marvelous it may seem today, will remain forever inexplicable. Soon or late the laws governing the production of life itself will be discovered in the laboratory, and man may set up business as a creator on his own account. The thing, indeed, is not only conceivable; it is even highly probable. When it comes to pass the theologians will be staggered, but I do not go so far as to predict that they will be undone. More than once in the past, seeing this miracle or that suddenly transformed into an ordinary marvel, responsive to lowly natural laws, they have edged out of disaster by abandoning it quietly and turning to another. Their art and mystery will be secure so long as the supply holds out, and that, no doubt, will be a long time.

Their effort to occupy all the areas not yet conquered by science—in other words, their bold claim that what no one knows is their special province, that ignorance itself is a superior kind of knowledge, that their most fantastic guess must hold good until it is disproved—all this is certainly absurd enough, but even more absurd is their frequent attempt, just mentioned, to find support for their dogmas in what they allege to be overt facts.

What this process comes to in practice may be discovered by anyone who will go to the trouble to examine the common Christian evidences for the Resurrection and the Virgin Birth, or the Catholic proofs of the miracles of the saints, or the Fundamentalist Protestant demonstration that the solemn promise in Mark 16:18 may be relied upon, or the Mormon evidence that the Book of Mormon was written by Yahweh in person, on plates of gold.

Theological literature is largely given over to such ridiculous sophistries, and many of them are supported by multitudes of earnest witnesses. But all they really prove is that theologians are well aware, deep down in their hearts, that faith alone is not sufficient to make even half-wits believe in their mumbo-jumbo; they sense a need to sweeten the dose with such testimony as would convince a judge and jury. The result of their labors in that direction, continued through many centuries, has been only to reduce human reason to the quaking and malarious thing that it is today. They have gradually broken down all the natural barriers between fact and fiction, sense and nonsense, and converted logic into a weapon that mauls the truth far more often than it defends it.

John Stuart Mill

John Stuart Mill (1806-1873) is noted for three things. He was one of the greatest minds of all time; he was one of the greatest child prodigies of all time; and he was that rare phenomenon, a child reared without religion of any sort.

He began reading Greek at three. He was apologetic about not starting to read Latin until he was eight. Then, under the strict tutelage of his father, James Mill, the historian, he plowed through the *Bucolics* of Vergil; the first six books of the *Aeneid*; all of Horace except the *Epodes;* the *Fables* of Phaedrus; the first five books of Livy; all of Sallust; a considerable part of Ovid's *Metamorphoses;* some plays of Terence; two or three books of Lucretius; the *Iliad* and the *Odyssey;* one or two plays of Sophocles, Euripedes, and Aristophanes; all of Thucydides; a great part of Demosthenes, Eschines, and Lysias; and Aristotle's *Rhetoric.*

But his early reading lists did not include the Bible. "I was brought up from the first," he says in his *Autobiography*, "without any religious belief in the ordinary acceptation of the term. My father, educated in the creed of Scotch presbyterianism, had by his own studies and reflections been early led to reject not only the belief in revelation, but the foundation of what is commonly called Natural Religion."

Was this neglect of religion by the elder Mill due to any lack of morality on his part? Critics of James Mill severely condemn him as a godless father who neglected his son's moral welfare. But John Stuart Mill indignantly rejected this charge and insisted that his father's faith, or lack of faith, was based on the highest morality. Here is the younger Mill's defense of his father's morality, taken from his *Autobiography* (first published in 1873).

—P.B.

Growing Up Without God

Those who admit an omnipotent as well as perfectly just and benevolent maker and ruler of such a world as this, can say little against Christianity but what can, with at least equal force, be retorted against themselves. Finding, therefore, no halting place in Deism, he [Mill's father] remained in a state of perplexity, until, doubtless after many struggles, he yielded to the conviction that, concerning the origin of things nothing whatever can be known.

This is the only correct statement of his opinion; for dogmatic atheism he looked upon as absurd, as most of those, whom the world has considered Atheists, have always done. These particulars are important, because they show that my father's rejection of all that is called religious belief was not, as many might suppose, primarily a matter of logic and evidence; the grounds of it were moral, still more than intellectual. He found it impossible to believe that a world as full of evil was the work of an Author combining infinite power with perfect goodness and righteousness. His intellect spurned the subtleties by which men attempt to blind themselves to this open contradiction. . . .

As it was, his aversion to religion, in the sense usually attached to the term, was of the same kind as that of Lucretius; he regarded it with the feeling due not a mere mental delusion, but to a great moral evil. He looked upon it as the greatest enemy of morality; first by setting up factitious excellencies—belief in creeds, devotional feelings, and ceremonies, not connected with the good of human kind—and causing these to be accepted as substitutes for genuine virtues; but above all, by radically vitiating the standard of morals, making it consist in doing the will of a being, on whom it lavishes indeed all the phrases of adulation, but whom in sober truth it depicts as eminently hateful.

I have a hundred times heard him say that all ages and nations have represented their gods as wicked, in a constantly increasing progression, that mankind have gone on adding trait after trait till they reached the most perfect conception of wickedness which the human mind can devise, and have called this God, and prostrated themselves before it. This *ne plus ultra* of wickedness he considered to be embodied in what is commonly presented to mankind as the creed of Christianity. Think (he used to say) of a being who would make a hell—who would create the human race with the infallible foreknowledge, and therefore with the intention—that the great majority of them were to be consigned to horrible and everlasting torment.

The time, I believe, is drawing near when this dreadful conception of an object of worship will no longer be identified with Christianity; and when all persons, with any sense of moral good and evil, will look upon it with the same indignation with which my father regarded it. . . . The world would be astonished if it knew how great a proportion of its brightest ornaments—of those most distinguished even in popular estimation for wisdom and virtue—are complete skeptics in religion.

The Nation

The recent death of Freda Kirchwey, former editor and publisher of *The Nation*, should serve to remind the public that she was once the heroine of a great battle for the speech on religion. I refer to the battle over the ban of *The Nation* from the public-school libraries of New York City in retaliation for the publication of several articles criticizing the policies of the Roman Catholic Church.

I was the unwilling victim of that ban because I had written the articles in question, but Freda was the heroine. It was she who organized the ad hoc committee of protest, headed by Archibald MacLeish, which included the greatest collection of American literary leaders ever assembled in such a movement, and it was she who was chiefly responsible for issuing a charter of intellectual freedom that defended the right of Americans to speak candidly about religion even when their speech offended some devotees of their faith.

Freda's own views about Catholicism were cheerfully critical—she had once said: "We believe the church is today the most potent organized force opposing freedom and progress in this country." But she kept her sights high in the drive against *The Nation*, refraining from any anticlerical emphasis and publishing much rebuttal material.

Reproduced below is part of the "Appeal to Reason and Conscience," written by MacLeish's committee of protest and printed in the October 16, 1948 issue of *The Nation*. I have appended, by way of illustration, the names of thirty-nine leading intellectuals who approved the fight against the ban. (The total list of more than one hundred names is too voluminous to be included here.)

The Nation's long battle against the ban ended in technical defeat in New York courts, and the magazine was not restored to New York's school-library shelves until many years later, after the journal had changed ownership. New York's highest court, the Court of Appeals, was at that time operating under an outrageously partisan interpretation of religious freedom, which it expressed thus: "No religion . . . shall be treated with contempt, mockery, scorn or ridicule." In defeat, Freda scored a moral victory. She served notice on the Catholic bishops that they could not, in spite of their great political power, successfully impose clerical censorship on American culture. The bishops carefully avoided direct participation in the ban, but their attitudes became dreadfully apparent a few months later when Cardinal Spellman attacked Eleanor Roosevelt because of her "documents of discrimination unworthy of an American mother," which included her participation in the Ad Hoc Committee to Lift the Ban on *The Nation*.

Freda's long fight for the right to criticize a religion has borne rich fruit within the Catholic Church itself. Canon 1399 of Catholic Canon Law, that notorious canon that forbids any Catholic to read a book directly attacking Catholic faith, is now virtually a dead letter. American church leaders, after *The Nation's* "defeat," have realized that such suppression is counterproductive in a free society.

—P.B.

Appeal to Reason and Conscience

On June 8 the Board of Superintendents of New York City's schools closed the schools to *The Nation*, the oldest liberal magazine in the United States. This action was taken without advance notice to *The Nation* or to the people of the city, without a hearing and without announcement of any kind, either to the magazine or to the public. The only opportunity afforded to the magazine to defend itself or to citizens to be heard, was at a meeting of the board from which the press was excluded, and which was called as a result of public protest some weeks after the decision had accidentally become known. After this proceeding, the board reaffirmed its decision by unanimous vote.

Other communities thereupon followed suit by similar unilateral action. In Massachusetts *The Nation* was banned from the State Teachers' Colleges by a public official who admitted he had not, at the time of the banning, himself investigated the reason given by the New York board for its action.

That reason was the publication by *The Nation* in 1947 and 1948 of a series of articles by Paul Blanshard, for many years Commissioner of Investigations and Accounts of the City of New York in the LaGuardia administration. Mr. Blanshard's articles described and criticized the official position of the Catholic Church in such matters as education, science, medicine, marriage and divorce, democracy and fascism. The board stated that there were passages in these articles which a Catholic would find objectionable on grounds of faith.

It is the opinion of the undersigned that the action of The New York Board of Superintendents raises an issue of the greatest gravity to the people of the city and of the country. It is not an issue between Catholic and non-Catholic. There are Catholics among us, and none of us, whether Catholic or not, have been moved to protest by reason of hostility to the Catholic faith. Neither is the issue raised a mere issue of fact with regard to the articles themselves. We agree with the board that there are sincere Catholics and men of good will who object on grounds of faith to certain statements in Mr. Blanshard's articles. Indeed, some of us who are not Catholics, disagree with certain of Mr. Blanshard's statements.

The issue as we see it is the issue of principle which the board's action and the board's statements in defense of its action present. The question before the board was not the question of the suitability of *The Nation* as a textbook in the city's schools. The question was whether *The Nation*, which had long been one of the periodicals available to New York students, should continue to be available to them. In ruling that it should not, and in giving the publication of the Blanshard articles as justification, the board in effect enunicated two propositions, both of which in our opinion are contrary to American ideas of freedom and destructive of American principles.

The first is the proposition that any published material which is regarded, or which could be regarded, as objectionable on grounds of faith or creed by any group in the community should be excluded from the community's schools and school libraries.

The second is the proposition that the appearance in any publication of material of this kind justifies the suppression in schools and school libraries of the publication as a whole. In the case of a periodical this means that the past publication of such material justifies the suppression of future issues regardless of the general character and record of the periodical.

The vice of the second of these two propositions is apparent upon its face. The exclusion from public institutions, by public officials, of future issues of newspapers, magazines, or other periodicals on the basis of particular material published in the past, rather than on the basis of the character of the publication as a whole, cannot be defended even as censorship. It is extra-judicial punishment pure and simple, and it involves a power of intimidation and possible blackmail in officials of government which no free society can tolerate and which a free press could not long survive. To permit public officials, in their unlimited, extra-judicial discretion, to stigmatize an established and respected magazine or newspaper as unfit for students to read because of the publication of a specific article or series of articles, or of particular paragraphs in a specific article or series, is to confer an arbitrary and dictatorial power which is wholly foreign to the American tradition and to the laws and Constitution in which the American tradition is expressed.

The first proposition—that any publication objectionable on grounds of faith to any group in the community should be suppressed in the schools—though more plausible on its face, is equally vicious in fact. It is a repudiation, on one side, of the principle of freedom of education; on the other, of the principle of the separation of church and state. The meaning of that latter tenet, so far as education is concerned, is that no church may use the public schools as instruments of its propaganda. To give the churches of the country, or any of their members who might seek to exercise it, the power to determine by simple veto what shall *not* be available to students in the public schools, or, worse, for public officials to exclude automatically anything any group might be expected to wish excluded, is to do by negative action what the Constitution and the courts forbid by positive action.

The argument offered in defense of this revolutionary proposal is apparently that religion cannot be criticized in American education. There is nothing in American law or in the American tradition which says that religion cannot be criticized in education, nor does the principle of the separation of church and state involve any such consequence. On the contrary, the American Republic was founded, and the American continent was settled, by people whose actions were in large part an expression of their criticism of certain established religions. Criticism of religion can certainly take forms which are unsuitable to schools, just as political controversy can take forms which are the opposite of instructive. But the doctrine that the criticism of religion must be outlawed *as such* in American education is a proposition which has no justification in American experience. Ignorance is notoriously the worst foundation for tolerance, and the American people have never felt that education should teach their children to be blind.

Archibald MacLeish, Eleanor Roosevelt, Herbert H. Lehman, Leonard Bernstein, Lillian Smith, Fannie Hurst, Cass Canfield, William Rose Benet, Henry Seidel Canby, G. Bromley Oxnam, Rex Stout, Max Lerner, Alvin Johnson, Bernard DeVoto, Dorothy Canfield Fisher, Oscar Hammerstein II, Sinclair Lewis, Lewis Mumford, Louis Untermeyer, Elmer Rice, Mark Van Doren, Sumner Welles, Stephen S. Wise, Edward R. Murrow, Reinhold Niebuhr, Allan Nevins, Bud Schulberg, Samuel Hopkins Adams, Truman Capote, Langston Hughes, Henry Steele Commager, Henry Emerson Fosdick, Virginia Gildersleeve, Hamilton Holt, Robert Hutchins, Howard Mumford Jones, Frank P. Graham, Perry Miller, Albert Spalding, Marshall Field III

Thomas Paine

Although Thomas Paine has become the most famous freethinker in American history, he was by no means a consistent critic of all religion. He was, at heart, a sentimental deist who believed in both God and immortality. He once proclaimed that "all religions are in their nature mild and benign," but he attacked the forms and fallacies of current religions with great ferocity. He was particularly caustic in dealing with Christianity.

Born in Thetford, England, the son of a Quaker, he had little formal education. After a poverty-stricken early manhood he came to America at the age of thirty-seven with letters of introduction from Benjamin Franklin. Almost immediately he embarked on a great American career as a pamphleteer. It was apparent that he had a gift for writing for the common man. In 1776 he published his pamphlet, *Common Sense,* a plea for an American republic. It was, perhaps, the most influential publication of the period.

Returning to Europe for a time, Paine wrote brilliantly in defense of the French Revolution, was thrown into a French prison and narrowly escaped execution. During his ten months in prison he completed his most controversial work, *The Age of Reason, Being an Investigation of True and Fabulous Theology.* Instantly he was attacked as a crude and irresponsible infidel. The world was not yet ready for his kind of honesty.

Actually, Paine considered himself a sincere opponent of atheism and a defender of honest faith. "I believe in one God and no more," he said, "and I hope for happiness beyond this life." These positive aspects of Paine's opinions were promptly forgotten by his critics.

When Paine returned to the United States, although Jefferson invited him to the Executive Mansion, he was assailed in American newspapers as a "drunken atheist" and "an object of disgust." When he died at seventy-two, the Quakers refused to bury him in their cemetery.

Paine was the first English writer of distinction to attack the Christian gospel of salvation in language that the common man could understand. This seemed equivalent to treason in the eyes of the British upper classes. In England, several of Paine's publishers were sent to prison— one went for three years and another was made to stand in a pillory in the streets once a month.

Paine preserved an almost naive faith in the intelligence of his readers. In his introduction to *The Age of Reason* in 1794 he wrote:

> TO MY FELLOW CITIZENS OF THE UNITED STATES
> OF AMERICA
>
> I put the following work under your protection. It contains my opinion upon religion. You will do me the justice to remember that I have always supported the right of every man to his opinion, however different that opinion might be to mine. He who denies to another this right makes a slave of himself to his present opinion because he precludes himself the right of changing it.
>
> The most formidable weapon against errors of every kind is reason. I have never used any other, and I trust I never shall.
>
> Your affectionate friend and fellow citizen,
>
> THOMAS PAINE

I have chosen the four following extracts from *The Age of Reason.*
—P.B.

The Creed
of a Skeptical Deist

I believe in one God, and no more; and I hope for happiness beyond this life. I believe in the equality of man; and I believe that religious duties consist in doing justice, loving mercy, and endeavoring to make our fellow-creatures happy.

But, lest it be supposed that I believe many other things in addition to these, I shall, in the progress of this work, declare the things I do not believe, and my reasons for not believing them.

I do not believe in the creed professed by the Jewish Church, by the Roman Church, by the Greek Church, by the Turkish Church, by the Protestant Church, nor by any church that I know of. My own mind is my own church. . . .

Do we want to contemplate His power? We see it in the immensity of the Creation. Do we want to contemplate His wisdom? We see it in the unchangeable order by which the imcomprehensible whole is governed. Do we want to contemplate His munificence? We see it in the abundance with which He fills the earth. Do we want to contemplate His mercy? We see it in His not withholding that abundance even from the unthankful. In fine, do we want to know what God is? Search the Scripture called the Creation.

Miracles and Prophecy

If we are to suppose a miracle to be something so entirely out of the course of what is called nature, that she must go out of that course to accomplish it, and we see an account given of such miracle by the person who said he saw it, it raises a question in the mind very easily decided, which is, is it more probable that nature should go out of her course, or that a man should tell a lie?

We have never seen, in our time, nature go out of her course; but we have good reason to believe that millions of lies have been told in the same time; it is, therefore, at least millions to one, that the reporter of a miracle tells a lie.

The story of the whale swallowing Jonah, though a whale is large enough to do it, borders greatly on the marvellous; but it would have approached nearer to the idea of miracle if Jonah had swallowed the whale. In this, which may serve for all cases of miracles, the matter would decide itself, namely is it more probable that a man should have swallowed a whale or told a lie. . . .

The most extraordinary of all the things called miracles related in the New Testament is that of the devil flying away with Jesus Christ, and carrying him to the top of a high mountain; and to the top of the highest pinnacle of the temple, and showing him and promising to him all the kingdoms of the world. How happened it that he did not discover America; or is it only with kingdoms that his sooty highness has any interest?

I have too much respect for the moral character of Christ to believe that he told this whale of a miracle himself; neither is it easy to account for what purpose it could have been fabricated, unless it were to impose upon the connoisseurs of miracles, as is sometimes practised upon the connoisseurs of Queen Anne's fair things, and collectors of relics and antiquities; or to render the belief of miracles ridiculous by outdoing miracles, as Don Quixote outdid chivalry; or to embarrass the belief of miracles by making it doubtful by what power, whether of God or of the devil, anything called a miracle was performed. . . .

As mystery and miracle took charge of the past and the present, prophesy took charge of the future, and rounded the tenses of faith. It was sufficient to know what had been done, but what would be done. The supposed prophet was the supposed historian of times to come; and if he happened, in shooting with a long bow of a thousand years, to strike within a thousand miles of a mark, the ingenuity of posterity could make it point-blank; and if he happened to be directly wrong, it was only to suppose, as in the case of Jonah and Ninevah, that God had repeated himself and changed his mind. What a fool do fabulous systems make of man!

Clerical Lying

All national institutions of churches, whether Jewish, Christian or Turkish, appear to me no other than human inventions, set up to terrify and enslave mankind, and monopolize power and profit.

I do not mean by this declaration to condemn those who believe otherwise; they have the same right to their belief as I have to mine. But it is necessary to the happiness of man that he be mentally faithful to himself. Infidelity does not consist in believing, or in disbelieving; it consists in professing to believe what he does not believe.

It is impossible to calculate the moral mischief, if I may so express it, that mental lying has produced in society. When a man has so far corrupted and prostituted the chastity of his mind as to subscribe his professional belief to things he does not believe, he has prepared himself for the commission of every other crime.

He takes up the profession of a priest for the sake of gain, and in order to qualify himself for that trade he begins with a perjury. Can we conceive anything more destructive to morality than this?

Wickedness in the Bible

Take away from Genesis the belief that Moses was the author, on which only the strange belief that it is the word of God has stood, and there remains nothing of Genesis but an anonymous book of stories, fables, and traditionary or invented absurdities, or of downright lies. The story of Eve and the serpent, and of Noah and his ark, drops to a level with the Arabian tales, without the merit of being entertaining; and the account of men living to eight and nine hundred years becomes as fabulous as the immortality of the giants of the Mythology.

Besides, the character of Moses, as stated in the Bible, is the most horrid that can be imagined. If those accounts be true, he

was the wretch that first began and carried on wars on the score
or on the pretence of religion; and under that mask, or that infat-
uation, committed the most unexampled atrocities that are to be
found in the history of any nation, of which I will state only one
instance.

When the Jewish army returned from one of their plundering
and murdering excursions, the account goes on as follows: Numbers, 31:13:

"And Moses, and Eleazar the priest, and all the princes of
the congregation, went forth to meet them without the camp; and
Moses was wroth with the officers of the host, with the captains
over thousands, and captains over hundreds, which came from
the battle; and Moses said unto them, '*Have ye saved all the
women alive?*' behold, these caused the children of Israel, through
the council of Balaam, to commit trespass against the Lord in the
matter of Peor, and there was a plague among the congregation of
the Lord. Now, therefore, *kill every male among the little ones,
and kill every woman that hath known a man by lying with him;
but all the women-children, that have not known a man by lying
with him, keep alive for yourselves.*"

Among the detestable villains that in any period of the world
have disgraced the name of man, it is impossible to find a greater
than Moses, if this account be true. Here is an order to butcher
the boys, to massacre the mothers, and debauch the daughters.

Let any mother put herself in the situation of those mothers;
one child murdered, another destined to violation, and herself in
the hands of an executioner; let any daughter put herself in the
situation of those daughters, destined as a prey to the murderers
of a mother and a brother, and what will be their feelings? It is in
vain that we attempt to impose upon nature, for nature will have
her course, and the religion that tortures all her social ties is a
false religion.

After this detestable order, follows an account of the plunder
taken, and the manner of dividing it; and here it is that the pro-
faneness of priestly hypocrisy increases the catalogue of crimes.
Verses 37 to 40: "*And the Lord's tribute* of the sheep was six
hundred and three score and fifteen; and the beeves were thirty
and six thousand, of which the *Lord's tribute* was three score and

twelve; and the asses were thirty thousand and five hundred, of which the Lord's tribute was three score and one; and the persons were sixteen thousand, of which the Lord's tribute was thirty and two persons." In short, matters contained in this chapter, as well as in many other parts of the Bible, are too horrid for humanity to read or for decency to hear, for it appears, from this thirty-fifth verse, that the number of women-children consigned to debauchery by the order of Moses was thirty-two thousand.

People in general do not know what wickedness there is in this pretended word of God. Brought up in habits of superstition, they take it for granted that the Bible is true, and that it is good; they permit themselves not to doubt of it, and they carry the ideas they form of the benevolence of the Almighty to the book which they have been taught to believe was written by his authority. Good heavens! it is quite another thing; it is a book of lies, wickedness, and blasphemy; for what can be greater blasphemy than to ascribe the wickedness of man to the orders of the Almighty?

J. M. Robertson

Although the English rationalist historian, John Mackinnon Robertson (1856-1933), is relatively unknown to the current generation of Americans, he was one of the most popular and prolific free-thought writers of his period. Our Library of Congress Index Catalogue still carries eighty-one titles by him, ranging over an astonishing variety of subjects in which Robertson had made himself an expert. In addition to his writing, Robertson had scored some successes in political life, being both an M.P. and a Right Honorable.

Robertson was ahead of his time among religious historians in practicing candor. He did not omit the Christian massacres, the inflation of holy myths, the exploitation of profitable indulgences and the papal confiscation of secular land. He described the Reformation as largely a struggle over monetary power, and he wrote a searching book called *The Jesus Problem* which anticipated many of the revelations now described as "demythologizing."

This may be an appropriate place for an American free-thought author to salute the great English free-thought conglomerate: The Thinker's Library, promoted by the English Rationalist Press Association and published by C. A. Watts and Company of London. This combination produced, in hundreds of cheap editions, the works of such eminent writers and scholars as H. G. Wells, Ernst Haeckel, Herbert Spencer, Charles Darwin, John Stuart Mill, Llewelyn Powys, Anatole France, T. H. Huxley and Leslie Stephen. Robertson was one of the favorites in this company. Would that America had ever produced such a fountain of wisdom and free thought!

I cannot refrain from special mention of one Thinker's Library best-seller which has proved to be a gold mine for me, *The Churches and Modern Thought* by Vivian Phelips.

I have chosen two selections from J. M. Robertson, both published by Watts, the first from his *Short History of Christianity*, the second from his *The Dynamics of Religion*.

—P.B.

The Crusades

The conventional view as to Christianity having been an abnormally efficient cause for good is a delusion. It is not Christianity that has civilized Europe, but Europe—the complex of political and cultural forces—that has partly civilized Christianity. . . .

That some social gains may be correlative with great historic evils is perhaps best seen in the case of the Crusades organized by the Church against the Saracens in Palestine. These campaigns were first conceived in the interest of the papal power. . . . Not, however, till Europe was full of tales of the cruelties wrought by the new Eastern power, the Turks, against Christian pilgrims—a marked change from the comparative tolerance of the Caliphs— was it possible to begin a vast crusading movement among all classes, aiming at the recovery of the empty sepulchre from which the Christ had risen. To this movement Pope Urban II zealously lent himself, backing up the wild appeal of Peter the Hermit (1094) with the fatal bribe of indulgences.

The first effect (1096) was to collect several immense and almost formless mobs of men and women who, by all accounts, were in the main the refuse of Christian Europe. . . . The devout exaltation of the few was submerged by the riot of the many, who began using their indulgences when they began their march, and rolled like a flood across Europe, massacring, torturing, and plundering Jews wherever they found them, and forcibly taking food where plunder was easy. Multitudes perished by the way; and multitudes more were sold as slaves in Byzantium to pay for the feeding of the rest there; and of the seven thousand who reached Asiatic soil with Peter the Hermit, four thousand were slain by the Turks at Nicea; some three hundred thousand thus perishing in all. Inasmuch as Europe was thus rid of a mass of its worst inhabitants, the first crusade might be said so far to have wrought indirect good; but the claim is hardly one to be pushed on righteous grounds.

The more organized military forces who soon followed under Godfrey of Bouillon and other leaders, though morally not better witnesses to Christianity, achieved at length (1099) the capture of Jerusalem, and founded the Latin kingdom of Palestine, which subsisted in force for less than a hundred years, and in a nominal form for a century longer.

As a display of Christian against "pagan" life and conduct, the process of conquest was worse than anything seen in the East in the Christian era. No armies were ever more licentious than those of "the cross"; and those of Attila were hardly more ferocious. Their own lives were lost in myriads, by the sword, by disease, and by debauchery. . . . [T]he one force to unify them was the hatred against the infidel, which wrecked itself in the massacre of men, women and children after the capture of a city. Beseiging Antioch, they shot heads of slain Turks into the city from their engines, and dug up hundreds of corpses to put the heads on pikes.

It is even recorded that when their savage improvidence left them starving at the seige of Mara they fed on the corpses they dug up. . . . When Godfrey took Jerusalem, the Jews there were all burned alive in their synagogues. . . . Thus was retrieved the mythic Savior's sepulchre.

Eight times during two hundred years was the effort repeated. . . . Till the end, no religious teacher seems to have doubted the fitness of the undertaking. St. Bernard preached the second Crusade as zealously as Peter did the first; eloquent monks were found, as they were needed, to rouse enthusiasm for each of the rest in turn; and King Louis IX of France, the model monarch of Christendom, saw his vain expedition to recover Jerusalem (1248) as the highest service to God or man. . . .

Among other fruits of the movement had been a vast increase in the papal revenues but . . . the crusading spirit died out in the thirteenth century. To all who could sanely judge, it had become clear that the crusades were at once a vast drain on the blood and treasure of Europe, and a vast force of demoralization. . . .

Christendom thenceforth crusaded with its tongue in its cheek. From the first the papacy had taught that no faith need be kept with unbelievers; and so was given a very superfluous apprenticeship to bad faith between Christians. When in 1212 there broke out the hapless Children's Crusades, out of the thirty thousand who followed the boy Stephen some way through France, five thousand were shipped at Marseilles by merchants who, professing to carry them "for the cause of God, and without charge," sold them as slaves at Algiers and Alexandria. The last recruits furnished by Pope Nicholas IV to the Grand Master of the Templars were drawn from the jails of Italy. It is a reasonable calculation that in the two centuries from the first crusade to the fall of Acre (1291) there had perished, in the attempts to recover and hold the Holy Land, nine millions of human beings, at least half of them Christians.

The Futility of Missions

Already the derisive hostility of laymen to the machinery of missions has gone so far that one may hazard a prediction of serious trouble accruing of the churches on this score before another generation passes. The blank futility of mission expenditure, on the missioners' own showing and from the believers' point of view, is now generally recognized among the working class; and the temerity with which the clergy still carry on the game is almost surprising.

At a recent meeting of the Church Missionary Society they went through the form of earnestly praying to their Deity to do as regards the Indian Famine what seemed to him to be fit; and they actually went on to profess a belief that their operations will ere long convert the entire population of India to Christ. To plain people, who have read the grieved avowal of the more sincere supervisors of mission work in India that the higher education of natives under missionary auspices simply produces unbelievers, this method of obtaining funds is not readily to be distinguished from lay swindling. And, as the stress of the struggle for life heightens, and the criticism of society progresses on quasi-Socialist lines, the huge revenues still obtainable for missionary enterprise are likely to dwindle disastrously, with the result of shaking clerical credit in other ways. They are largely obtained from women and from capitalists; but women are becoming yearly more accessible to social science, and capitalists are becoming yearly more open to social criticism.

Eleanor Roosevelt

At first glance the famous 1949 quarrel between Mrs. Eleanor Roosevelt and Cardinal Spellman over tax grants to parochial schools does not qualify as a classic of free thought. Mrs. Roosevelt was far from being a freethinker, and her exchanges with Cardinal Spellman were replete with expressions of conventional Christian faith. She was a sincere and sentimental Protestant. In one of her *My Day* columns she had said: "I have no feeling against the use of a prayer which all children of all denominations could say in the public school." (This was exactly the kind of prayer which was later outlawed as unconstitutional by the Supreme Court.)

Although the Roosevelt-Spellman controversy was nominally a minor quarrel over public money; it became, because of the prominence of the participants and the prodigious publicity, a quarrel over fundamental values in American political and religious freedom. Mrs. Roosevelt, in expressing her thoughts, was defending the American tradition against European clerical policy, and she became, willy nilly, the national symbol of the American style of religious liberty. She also became the symbol of the American style of public education as against the Catholic style of education in continental Europe when she said: "Anyone who knows history, particularly the history of Europe, will, I think, recognize that the domination of education or of government by any one particular religious faith is never a happy arrangement for the people."

Most of the public seemed to take Mrs. Roosevelt's side in the controversy. This was bitter medicine for the cardinal. He was not accustomed to the villian's role. After the attached letters had appeared in print, he came to Eleanor's house, hat in hand, and made amends for suggesting that she might be an unworthy American mother. Although his penance was personal, there is no doubt that it was directed by the Vatican. Pius XII was horrified that a leader of his Church should be pitted against so famous a world heroine.

The Spellman-Roosevelt controversy had really been going on semi-

143

publicly for some time. Graham Barden of North Carolina had, after years of Catholic sabotage, succeeded in getting before Congress a bill for appropriating three hundred million dollars for public schools without any corresponding appropriation for parochial schools. Cardinal Spellman and his associates had brought terrific pressure to bear on Congress against the Barden bill. In effect the Catholic hierarchy had said: "Vote us tax funds also or else. . . . " The "else" was the threat to attack the public school system as godless or pro-Communist. A few weeks after the Roosevelt-Spellman exchange, the leading American-Catholic newspaper, *Our Sunday Visitor*, declared: "Most non-Catholics know that the Catholic schools are rendering a greater service to our nation than the public schools in which subversive textbooks have been used, in which Communist-minded teachers have taught, and from whose classrooms Christ and even God Himself are barred."

In the exchange Mrs. Roosevelt was bland and dignified. Spellman was not even superficially truthful. The cardinal pretended that all his Church wanted was fringe benefits. The whole history of Catholic demands upon the public treasury in the United States and abroad belies this claim. Indeed, Spellman himself demanded full financial equality for Catholic schools as soon as a Catholic president entered the White House. The parochial school system, paid for with public money but controlled by the Church as an organic part of that Church, is the worldwide goal of Catholic educational policy. This is the approved scheme of financing Catholic education as sanctioned by Catholic Canon Law.

I have reprinted the entire text of Mrs. Roosevelt's *My Day* column of June 23, 1949, Cardinal Spellman's attack of July 21, and Mrs. Roosevelt's reply of July 23.

—P.B.

The Spellman-Roosevelt Exchange

The controversy brought about by the request made by Francis Cardinal Spellman that Catholic schools should share in federal aid funds forces upon the citizens of the country the kind of decision that is going to be very difficult to make.

Those of us who believe in the right of any human being to belong to whatever church he sees fit, and to worship God in his own way, cannot be accused of prejudice when we do not want to see public education connected with religious control of the schools, which are paid for by taxpayers' money.

If we desire our children to go to schools of any particular kind, be it because we think they should have religious instruction or for any other reason, we are entirely free to set up those schools and to pay for them. Thus, our children would receive the kind of education we feel would best fit them for life.

Many years ago it was decided that the public schools of our country should be entirely separated from any kind of denominational control, and these are the only schools that are free, tax-supported schools. The greatest number of our children attend these schools.

It is quite possible that private schools, whether they are denominational schools—Catholic, Episcopalian, Presbyterian, Methodist, or whatever—or whether they are purely academic, may make a great contribution to the public school systems, both on the lower levels and on the higher levels.

They will be somewhat freer to develop new methods and to try experiments, and they will serve as yardsticks in the competitive area of creating better methods of imparting knowledge.

This, however, is the very reason why they should not receive federal funds; in fact, no tax funds of any kind.

The separation of church and state is extremely important to any of us who hold to the original traditions of our nation. To change these traditions by changing our traditional attitude toward public education would be harmful, I think, to our whole attitude of tolerance in the religious area.

If we look at situations which have arisen in the past in Europe and other world areas, I think we will see the reasons why it is wise to hold to our early traditions.

Cardinal Spellman

Dear Mrs. Roosevelt:

When, on June 23 in your column, "My Day," you aligned yourself with the author and other proponents of the Barden bill and condemned me for defending Catholic children against those who would deny them their constitutional rights of equality with other American children, you could have acted only from misinformation, ignorance or prejudice, not from knowledge and understanding.

It is apparent that you did not take the time to read my address delivered at Fordham University; and, in your column of July 15 you admitted that you did not even carefully read and acquaint yourself with the facts of the Barden bill—the now famous, infamous bill that would unjustly discriminate against minority groups of America's children.

Unlike you, Mrs. Roosevelt, I did not make a public statement until I had studied every phrase of the Barden bill; nor did I take issue with a man because his faith differed from mine. We differed, Congressman Barden and I, over the unimpeachable issue of equal benefits and equal rights for all America's children.

I had intended ignoring your personal attack, but, as the days passed and in two subsequent columns you continued your anti-Catholic campaign, I became convinced that it was in the interest of all Americans and the cause of justice itself that your misstatements should be challenged in every quarter of our country where they have already spun and spread their web of prejudice. I have received hundreds of messages from persons of all faiths demanding that I answer you. I am, therefore, not free to ignore you.

You say you are against religious control of schools which are paid for by taxpayers' money. That is exactly what I, too, oppose. But I am also opposed to any bill that includes children who attend parochial schools for the purpose of receiving funds from the federal government while it excludes these same children from the distribution and benefits of the funds allocated.

I believe that if the federal government provides a bottle of milk to each child in a public school it should provide milk for all school children. I believe if, through the use of federal funds the children who attend public schools are immunized from contagious diseases that all children should be protected from these diseases.

"Taxation without representation" is tyranny was the cry that roused and rallied our pioneer Americans to fight for justice. Taxation without participation should rouse today's Americans to equal ardor to protest an injustice that would deprive millions of American children of health and safety benefits to which all our children are entitled. And the Supreme Court of the United States has declared that health and transportation services and the distribution of nonreligious textbooks to pupils attending parochial schools do not violate our Constitution.

"The separation of church and state is extremely important to us who hold to the original traditions of our nation," you continue. But health and safety benefits and providing standard nonreligious textbooks for all American children have nothing to do with the question of separation of church and state!

I cannot presume upon the press to discuss, analyze or refute each inaccuracy in your columns—for they are manifold. Had you taken an objective, impersonal stand, I could then, in the same impersonal manner, answer you. But you did not. Apparently your attitude of mind precluded you from comprehending issues which you either rigorously defended or flagrantly condemned while ignorant of the facts concerning both the Barden bill and my own denunciation of it.

American freedom not only permits but encourages differences of opinion and I do not question your right to differ with me. But why, I wonder, do you repeatedly plead causes that are anti-Catholic?

Even if you cannot find it within your heart to defend the rights of innocent little children and heroic, helpless men like Cardinal Martyr Mindszenty, can you not have the charity not to cast upon them still another stone?

America's Catholic youth helped fight a long and bitter fight to save all Americans from oppression and persecution. Their broken bodies on blood-soaked foreign fields were grim and tragic testimony of this fact. I saw them there—on every fighting front—as equally they shared with their fellow-fighters all the sacrifice, terror and gore of war—as alike they shared the little good and glory that sometimes comes to men as together they fight and win a brutal battle.

Would you deny equality to these Catholic boys who daily stood at the sad threshold of untimely death and suffered martyrdom that you and I and the world of men might live in liberty and peace?

Would you deny their children equal rights and benefits with other sects—rights for which their fathers paid equal taxation with other fathers and fought two bitter wars that all children might forever be free from fear, oppression and religious persecution?

During the war years you visited the hospitals in many countries, as did I. You too saw America's sons—Catholic, Protestant and Jew alike—young, battered, scarred, torn and mutilated, dying in agony that we might learn to live in charity with one another. Then how was it that your own heart was not purged of all prejudices by what you saw these, your sons, suffer?

Now my case is closed. This letter will be released to the public tomorrow after it has been delivered to you by special delivery today. And even though you may again use your columns to attack me and again accuse me of starting a controversy, I shall not again publicly acknowledge you. For, whatever you may say in the future, your record of anti-Catholicism stands for all to see— a record which you yourself wrote on the pages of history which cannot be recalled—documents of discrimination unworthy of an American mother!

Sincerely yours,

FRANCIS CARDINAL SPELLMAN
Archbishop of New York

Mrs. Roosevelt

Your Eminence:

Your letter of July 21 surprised me considerably.

I have never advocated the Barden bill nor any other specific bill on education now before the Congress. I believe, however, in federal aid to education.

I have stated in my column some broad principles which I consider important and said I regretted your attack on the Barden bill because you aligned yourself with those who, from my point of view, advocated an unwise attitude which may lead to difficulties in this country, and have, as a result, the exact things which you and I would deplore, namely, the increase in bitterness among the Roman Catholic groups, and the Protestant and other religious groups.

I read only what was in the papers about your address and I stated in my column very carefully that I had not read the Barden bill or any other bill carefully, because I do not wish to have it said that I am in favor of any particular bill.

If I may, I would like to state again very simply for you the things I believe are important in this controversy. In the early days in this country there were rather few Roman Catholic settlements. The majority of the people coming here were Protestants and not very tolerant, but they believed that in establishing a democratic form of government it was essential that there be free education for as large a number of people as possible, so there was a movement to create free public schools for all children who wished to attend them. Nothing was said about private schools.

As we have developed in this country we have done more and more for our public schools. They are open to all children and it has been decided that there should be no particular religious beliefs taught in them.

I believe that there should be freedom for every child to be educated in his own religion. In public schools it should be taught that the spiritual side of life is most important. I would be happy if some agreement could be reached on passages from the Bible and some prayer that could be used. The real religious teaching of any child must be done by his own church and in his own home.

It is fallacious, I think, to say that because children going to public schools are granted free textbooks in some states, free transportation, or free school lunches, that these same things must be given to children going to private schools.

Different states, of course, have done different things as they came under majority pressure from citizens who had certain desires, but basically by and large, throughout the country, I think there is still a feeling that the public school is the school which is open to all children, and which is supported by all the people of the country and that anything that is done for the public schools should be done for them alone.

I would feel that certain medical care should be available to all children, but that is a different thing and should be treated differently. If we set up free medical care for all children, then it should not be tied in with any school.

At present there are physical examinations for children in public schools which are provided without cost to the parents, but there is nothing to prevent people who send their children to private schools from making arrangements to pay for similar examinations for their children.

I should like to point out to you that I talked about parochial schools and that to my mind means any schools organized by any sectarian group and not exclusively a Roman Catholic school. Children attending parochial schools are, of course, taught according to the tenets of their respective churches.

As I grow older it seems to me important that there be no great stress laid on our divisions, but that we stress as much as possible our agreements.

You state: "And the Supreme Court of the United States has declared that health and transportation services and the distribution of nonreligious textbooks to pupils attending parochial schools do not violate our Constitution." None of us will presume to decide questions which will come up before the Supreme Court of the United States, but all of us must think seriously about anything which is done, not only in relation to the specific thing, but in relation to what may follow after it and what we think will be good for the country.

Anyone who knows history, particularly the history of Europe, will, I think, recognize that the domination of education or of government by any one particular religious faith is never a happy arrangement for the people.

Spiritual leadership should remain spiritual leadership and the temporal power should not become too important in any church.

I have no bias against the Roman Catholic Church and I have supported Governor Smith as Governor and worked for him as a candidate for the office of President of the United States. I have supported for public office many other Roman Catholic candidates.

You speak of the Mindszenty case. I spoke out very clearly against any unfair type of trial and anything anywhere in any country which might seem like attack on an individual because of his religious beliefs. I cannot, however, say that in European countries the control by the Roman Catholic Church of great areas of land has always led to happiness for the people of those countries.

I have never visited hospitals and asked or thought about the religion of any boy in any bed. I have never in a military cemetery had any different feeling about the graves of the boys who lay there. All of our boys of every race, creed and color fought for the country and they deserve our help and gratitude.

It is not my wish to deny children anywhere equal rights or benefits. It is, however, the decision of parents when they select a private or denominational school, whether it be Episcopal, Wesleyan, Jewish, or Roman Catholic.

I can assure you that I have no prejudice. I understand the beliefs of the Roman Catholic Church very well. I happen to be a Protestant and I prefer my own church, but that does not make me feel that anyone has any less right to believe as his own convictions guide him.

I have no intention of attacking you personally, nor of attacking the Roman Catholic Church, but I shall, of course, continue to stand for the things in our government which I think are right. They may lead me to be in opposition to you and to other groups within our country, but I shall always act, as far as I am able, from real conviction and from honest belief.

If you carefully studied my record, I think you would not find it one of anti-Catholic or anti-any-religious group.

I assure you that I have no sense of being "an unworthy American mother." The final judgment, my dear Cardinal Spellman, of the worthiness of all human beings is in the hands of God.

With deepest respect, I am

Very sincerely yours,

ELEANOR ROOSEVELT
(MRS. FRANKLIN D. ROOSEVELT)

Bertrand Russell

Bertrand Arthur William Russell, 3d Earl (1872-1970) was a free-thought natural, a world-renowned philosopher who still wrote persuasively for the common man, and an opponent of organized religion who became a moral prophet without sanction of churches. Coming from one of England's most distinguished families, he was also distinguished as a social rebel, having served as a jail bird for his pacifism during World War I. He made a remarkable recovery in reputation during World War II. Before he died in his late nineties, England rewarded him with the Order of Merit, and the world cheered when he was given the Nobel prize for literature in 1950.

Russell was a prodigious worker, producing about three thousand almost-errorless words a day through a long career. At one time he had forty books on the market simultaneously, ranging from profound masterpieces on metaphysics to popular pamphlets on sexual morals.

It was in this latter field that he inadvertently gained his greatest American fame. Appointed by the educational authorities to the chair of philosophy at New York City College, Russell was made the victim of a highly organized right-wing campaign of vilification as a man who "specifically defends adultery"—see Paul Edward's account in the Appendix of Russell's *Why I Am Not a Christian*. The Jesuit magazine *America* called him "a dessicated, divorced, and decadent advocate of sexual promiscuity. . . . [A] professor of immorality and irreligion."

It is true that Russel was pretty advanced for the 1940s in both religion and sexuality. His 1929 book, *Marriage and Morals*, used plain words on the subject. He contended that sexual relations between unmarried people were not always wrong, and that occasional extra-marital relations were not necessarily grounds for divorce. This was too much for a conservative Catholic judge in New York who took the initiative against Russell. And I regret to say it was too much for Mayor Fiorello LaGuardia who was a puritan and at the same time a politician who needed the Catholic vote. With the silent collaboration of the mayor,

Russell's appointment to City College was blocked because the city funds for the chair were withheld. (I had completed my four-year stint in La-Guardia's cabinet at the time this happened; otherwise I certainly would have resigned in protest.)

But all this should have been considered irrelevant to Russell's appointment at City College. Russell was not asked to teach a course in marriage and morals, and he had no intention of overstepping the limits of his metaphysical assignments. He was asked to conduct courses in logic, mathematics, and science, areas in which he was brilliantly competent.

Officially, Russell was an agnostic or an atheist—he usually preferred the first description but did not run away from the second. He did stand for personal freedom in his sexual life. He had three wives plus and three divorces.

With the kind permission of Simon and Schuster I have chosen to reproduce two selections from this publisher's still-current—and important—book, *Why I Am Not a Christian*. The first selection is from Russell's 1925 essay "What I Believe"; the second is a brief 1952 piece called "Religion and Morals."

—P.B.

Sexual Freedom

Another way in which superstition damages education is through its influence on the choice of teachers. For economic reasons, a woman teacher must not be married; for moral reasons, she must not have extramarital sexual relations. And yet everybody who has taken the trouble to study morbid psychology knows that prolonged virginity is, as a rule, extraordinarily harmful to women, so harmful that, in a sane society, it would be severely discouraged in teachers. The restrictions imposed lead more and more to a refusal, on the part of energetic and enterprising women, to enter the teaching profession. This is all due to the lingering influence of superstitious asceticism.

At middle- and upper-class schools the matter is even worse. There are chapel services, and the care of morals is in the hands of clergymen.

Clergymen almost necessarily fail in two ways as teachers of morals. They condemn acts which do no harm and they condone acts which do great harm. They all condemn sexual relations between unmarried people who are fond of each other but not yet sure that they wish to live together all their lives. Most of them condemn birth control. None of them condemn the brutality of a husband who causes his wife to die of too-frequent pregnancies.

I knew a fashionable clergyman whose wife had nine children in nine years. The doctors told him that if she had another she would die. Next year she had another and died. No one condemned him; he retained his benefice and married again. So long as clergymen continue to condone cruelty and condemn innocent pleasure, they can only do harm as guardians of the morals of the young.

Another bad effect of superstition on education is the absence of instruction about the facts of sex. The main physiological facts ought to be taught quite simply and naturally before puberty at a time when they are not exciting. At puberty, the elements of an unsuperstitious sexual morality ought to be taught. Boys and girls should be taught that nothing can justify sexual intercourse unless there is mutual inclination. This is contrary to the teaching of the church, which holds that, provided the parties are married and the man desires another child, sexual intercourse is justified, however great may be the reluctance of the wife.

Boys and girls should be taught respect for each other's liberty; they should be made to feel that nothing gives one human being rights over another, and that jealousy and possessiveness kill love. They should be taught that to bring another human being into the world is a very serious matter, only to be undertaken when the child will have a reasonable prospect of health, good surroundings, and parental care. But they should also be taught methods of birth control, so as to insure that children shall only come when they are wanted. Finally, they should be taught the dangers of venereal disease, and the methods of prevention and cure. The increase of human happiness to be expected from sex education on these lines is immeasurable.

It should be recognized that, in the absence of children, sexual relations are a purely private matter, which does not concern either the state or the neighbors. Certain forms of sex which do not lead to children are at present punished by the criminal law: this is purely superstitious, since the matter is one which affects no one except the parties directly concerned. Where there are children, it is a mistake to suppose that it is necessarily to their interest to make divorce very difficult. Habitual drunkenness, cruelty, insanity, are grounds upon which divorce is necessary for the children's sake quite as much as for the sake of the wife or husband.

The peculiar importance attached, at present, to adultery is quite irrational. It is obvious that many forms of misconduct are more fatal to married happiness than an occasional infidelity. Masculine insistence on a child a year, which is not conventionally misconduct or cruelty, is the most fatal of all.

Moral rules ought not to be such as to make instinctive happiness impossible. Yet that is an effect of strict monogamy in a community where the numbers of the two sexes are very unequal. Of course, under such circumstances, the moral rules are infringed. But when the rules are such that they can only be obeyed by greatly diminishing the happiness of the community, and when it is better they should be infringed than observed, surely it is time that the rules were changed. If this is not done, many people who are acting in a way not contrary to the public interest are faced with the undeserved alternative of hypocrisy, which is a flattering tribute to its power; but elsewhere it has come to be recognized as an evil which we ought not lightly to inflict.

Religion and Morals

Many people tell us that without belief in God a man can be neither happy nor virtuous. As to virtue, I can speak only from observation, not from personal experience. As to happiness, neither experience nor observation has led me to think that believers are either happier or unhappier, on the average, than unbelievers. It is customary to find "grand" reasons for unhappiness, because it is easier to be proud if one can attribute one's misery to lack of faith than if one has to put it down to the liver. As to morality, a great deal depends upon how one understands that term. For my part, I think the important virtues are kindness and intelligence. Intelligence is impeded by any creed, no matter what; and kindness is inhibited by the belief in sin and punishment (this belief, by the way, is the only one that the Soviet government has taken over from orthodox Christianity).

There are various practical ways in which traditional morality interferes with what is socially desirable. One of these is the prevention of venereal disease. More important is the limitation of population. Improvements in medicine have made this matter far more important than it ever was before. If the nations and races which are still as prolific as the British were a hundred years ago do not change their habits in this respect, there is no prospect for mankind except war and destitution. This is known to every intelligent student, but it is not acknowledged by theological dogmatists.

I do not believe that a decay of dogmatic belief can do anything but good. I admit at once that new systems of dogma, such as those of the Nazis and the Communists, are even worse than the old systems, but they could never have acquired a hold over men's minds if orthodox dogmatic habits had not been instilled in youth. Stalin's language is full of reminiscences of the theological seminary in which he received this training. What the world needs is not dogma but an attitude of scientific inquiry combined with a belief that the torture of millions is not desirable, whether inflicted by Stalin or by a Deity imagined in the likeness of the believer.

Percy Bysshe Shelley

One of the most famous documents in the history of free thought is Percy Bysshe Shelley's small pamphlet *The Necessity of Atheism*. I reprint it here, not because it is effectively or brilliantly written, but because its suppression by Oxford authorities in 1811 made it a significant landmark in the battle for freedom of thought.

Shelley was only eighteen years old when he wrote this little philippic in conjunction with a fellow student at Oxford, Thomas Jefferson Hogg. Since he did not dare to sign his own name to the document, he used the pseudonym Jeremiah Stukeley. He sent a copy to "every bishop in the Kingdom . . . and the other heads of houses in Oxford," and in addition he pasted up atheistic slogans on the chapel door. When an Oxford book dealer offered the pamphlet for sale, it survived only twenty minutes. The college authorities swooped down on the store, seized all copies, and burned all except one.

When Shelley, who had already become known as "the ringleader in every species of mischief within our grave walls," was summoned to appear before the master and fellows of his college, he at first refused to admit authorship on the grounds that he could not be compelled to incriminate himself. But when he was asked to disavow the pamphlet entirely, and refused, he and his friend Hogg were summarily expelled. As Shelley wrote to his father, "No argument was publicly brought forward to disprove our reasoning." No argument was necessary, since in England at that time blasphemy was a legal offense, and the denial of God's existence was blasphemy.

In spite of his reputation as a wild young rebel, Shelley was a serious student of religion. As he said to his father after his expulsion from Oxford, "You will know that a train of reasoning and not any great profligacy has induced me to disbelieve the scriptures."

Shelley in his early years, according to his biographer André Maurois, liked the word *atheist* "because of its vigor. He loved to fling it in the face of bigotry." Shelley once remarked about his own past, "I was once an enthusiastic Deist, but never a Christian." His frail deism was summarized in an 1811 letter: "What then is God? It is a name which expresses the unknown cause, the suppositious origin of all existence. . . . In this sense I acknowledge a God, but merely a synonym for the existing power of existence."

—P.B.

The Necessity of Atheism

A close examination of the validity of the proofs adduced to support any proposition, has ever been allowed to be the only sure way of attaining truth, upon the advantages of which it is unnecessary to descant; our knowledge of the existence of a Deity is a subject of such importance that it cannot be too minutely investigated; in consequence of this conviction, we proceed briefly and impartially to examine the proofs which have been adduced. It is necessary first to consider the nature of Belief.

When a proposition is offered to the mind, it perceives the agreement or disagreement of the ideas of which it is composed. A perception of their agreement is termed belief, many obstacles frequently prevent this perception from being immediate, these the mind attempts to remove in order that the perception may be distinct. The mind is active in the investigation, in order to perfect the state of perception which is passive; the investigation being confused with the perception has induced many falsely to imagine that the mind is active in belief, that belief is an act of volition, in consequence of which it may be regulated by the mind; pursuing, continuing this mistake they have attached a degree of criminality to disbelief of which in its nature it is incapable; it is equally so of merit.

The strength of belief like that of every other passion is in proportion to the degrees of excitement.

The degrees of excitement are three.

The senses are the sources of all knowledge to the mind, consequently their evidence claims the strongest assent.

The decision of the mind founded upon our own experience derived from these sources, claims the next degree.

The experience of others which addresses itself to the former one, occupies the lowest degree.

Consequently no testimony can be admitted which is contrary to reason, reason is founded on the evidence of our senses.

Every proof may be referred to one of these three divisions; we are naturally led to consider what arguments we receive from each of them to convince us of the existence of a Diety.

First. The evidence of the senses. If the Diety should appear to us, if he should convince our senses of his existence; this revelation would necessarily command belief; those to whom the Deity has thus appeared, have the strongest possible conviction of his existence.

Reason claims the second place, it is urged that man knows that whatever is, must either have had a beginning or existed from all eternity, he also knows that whatever is not eternal must have had a cause. Where this is applied to the existence of the universe, it is necessary to prove that it was created, until that is clearly demonstrated, we may reasonably suppose that it has endured from all eternity. In a case where two propositions are diametrically opposite, the mind believes that which is less incomprehensible, it is easier to suppose that the Universe has existed from all eternity, than to conceive a being capable of creating it; if the mind sinks beneath the weight of one, is it an alleviation to increase the intolerability of the burden? The other argument which is founded upon a man's knowledge of his own existence, stands thus. . . . A man knows not only he now is, but that there was a time when he did not exist, consequently there must have been a cause. . . . But what does this prove? We can only infer from effects causes exactly adequate to those effects . . . But there certainly is a generative power which is effected by particular instruments; we cannot prove that it is inherent in these instruments, nor is the contrary hypothesis capable of demonstration; we admit that the generative power is incomprehensible, but to suppose that the same effect is produced by an eternal, omniscient, Almighty Being, leaves the cause in the obscurity, but renders it more incomprehensible.

The third and last degree of assent is claimed by Testimony . . . it is required that it should not be contrary to reason. . . . The testimony that the Deity convinces the senses of men of his existence can only be admitted by us, if our mind considers it less probable that these men should have been deceived, than that the Deity should have appeared to them . . . our reason can never admit the testimony of men, who not only declare that they were eye-witnesses of miracles but that the Deity was irrational, for he commanded that he should be believed, he proposed the highest rewards for faith, eternal punishments for disbelief . . . we can only command voluntary actions, belief is not an act of volition, the mind is even passive, from this it is evident that we have not sufficient testimony, or rather that testimony is insufficient, to prove the being of God, we have therefore shown that it cannot be deduced from reason . . . they who have been convinced by the evidence of the senses, they only can believe it.

From this it is evident that having no proofs from any of the three sources of conviction: the mind *cannot* believe the existence of a God, it is also evident that as belief is a passion of the mind, no degree of criminality can be attached to disbelief, they only are reprehensible who willingly neglect to remove the false medium thro' which their mind views the subject.

It is almost unnecessary to observe, that the general knowledge of the deficiency of such proof, cannot be prejudicial to society: Truth has always been found to promote the best interests of mankind. . . . Every reflecting mind must allow that there is no proof of the existence of a Deity.—Q.E.D.

Leslie Stephen

Leslie Stephen (1832-1904) was for many years the not-so-gentle knight of English upper-class culture. He dripped with scholarship, excelled in learned ridicule, was knighted—and he was the father of Virginia Woolf.

These miscellaneous achievements should not obscure his solid literary triumphs. He was for many years one of England's most noted literary essayists. He was joint editor of the *Dictionary of National Biography*, author of the *History of English Thought in the Eighteenth Century*, and during his best years he contributed at least twenty-four essays on moral and religious themes to such magazines as the *Fortnightly Review*, the *Cornhill Magazine*, and the *Nineteenth Century*.

Although he was at the opposite end of the social ladder from the proletarian agnostic, Charles Bradlaugh, he came to Bradlaugh's assistance very effectively when the latter was being excluded from the House of Commons for failure to profess belief in God. (See Bradlaugh.) During that controversy, Sir Leslie declared that "if atheism is to be used to express the state of mind in which God is identified with the unknowable, and theology is pronounced to be a collection of meaningless words about unintelligible chimeras, then I have no doubt, and I think few people doubt, that atheists are as plentiful as blackberries. . . . I have no fear of being contradicted when I say that a majority of the House of Commons is either infidel or sublimely tolerant of infidelity."

Although it was T. H. Huxley who created the word "agnosticism" in 1869, it was Leslie Stephen who gave the word popular prestige with his famous 1876 article in the *Fortnightly Review*, "An Agnostic's Apology." Leslie's agnosticism was expressed as a high moral principle. He could endorse what the British philosopher W. K. Clifford said, that "it is wrong always, everywhere and for everyone to believe anything upon insufficient evidence." It is a tribute to English culture that Stephen maintained his eminent position while challenging Christian culture openly.

I have chosen to use several long fragments from the 1876 article.

—P.B.

An Agnostic's Apology

The race collectively is agnostic, whatever may be the case with individuals. Newton might be certain of the truth of his doctrines, whilst other thinkers were still convinced of their falsity. It could not be said that the doctrines were certainly true, so long as they were doubted in good faith by competent reasoners. Newman may be as much convinced of the truth of his theology as Professor Huxley of its error. But speaking of the race, and not of the individual, there is no plainer fact in history than the fact that hitherto no knowledge has been attained. There is not a single proof of natural theology of which the negative has not been maintained as vigorously as the affirmative.

You tell us to be ashamed of professing ignorance. Where is the shame of ignorance in matters still involved in endless and hopeless controversy? Is it not rather a duty? Why should a lad who has just run the gauntlet of examinations and escaped to a country parsonage be dogmatic, when his dogmas are denounced as erroneous by half the philosophers of the world? . . .

The ancient difficulty which has perplexed men since the days of Job is this: Why are happiness and misery arbitrarily distributed? Why do the good so often suffer, and the evil so often flourish? The difficulty, says the determinist, arises entirely from applying the conception of justice where it is manifestly out of place. The advocate of free-will refuses this escape, and is perplexed by a further difficulty. Why are virtue and vice arbitrarily distributed? Of all the puzzles of this dark world, or of all forms of the one great puzzle, the most appalling is that which meets us at the corner of every street.

Look at the children growing up amidst moral poison; see

the brothel and the public-house turning out harlots and drunk-
ards by the thousand; at the brutalised elders preaching cruelty
and shamelessness by example; and deny, if you can, that lust
and brutality are generated as certainly as scrofula and typhus.
Nobody dares to deny it. All philanthropists admit it; and every
hope of improvement is based on the assumption that the moral
character is determined by its surroundings.

What does the theological advocate of free-will say to reconcile such a spectacle with our moral conceptions? Will God damn
all these wretches for faults due to causes as much beyond their
power as the shape of their limbs or as the orbits of the planets?
Or will He make some allowance? . . .

The Christian revelation makes statements which, if true, are
undoubtedly of the very highest importance. God is angry with
man. Unless we believe and repent we shall all be damned. It is
impossible, indeed, for its advocates even to say this without
instantly contradicting themselves. Their doctrine frightens them.
They explain in various ways that a great many people will be
saved without believing, and that eternal damnation is not eternal
nor damnation. It is only the vulgar who hold such views, and
who, of course, must not be disturbed in them; but they are not
for the intelligent. God grants "uncovenanted mercies"—that is,
He sometimes lets a sinner off, though He has not made a legal
bargain about it—an explanation calculated to exalt our conceptions of the Deity! . . .

If I were to assert that of every ten beings born into this world
nine would be damned, that all who refused to believe what they
did not hold to be proved, and all who sinned from overwhelming
temptation, and all who had not had the good-fortune to be the
subjects of a miraculous conversion or the recipients of a grace
conveyed by a magical charm, would be tortured to all eternity,
what would an orthodox theologian reply?

He could not say, "That is false"; I might appeal to the
highest authorities for my justification; nor, in fact, could he on
his own showing deny the possibility. Hell, he says, exists; he does
not know who will be damned; though he does know that all men
are by nature corrupt and liable to be damned if not saved by
supernatural grace. He might, and probably would, now say,

"That is rash. You have no authority for saying how many will be lost and how many saved: you cannot even say what is meant by hell or heaven: you cannot tell how far God may be better than His word, though you may be sure that He won't be worse than His word." And what is all this but to say, We know nothing about it? In other words, to fall back on Agnosticism. . . .

The whole world in which we live may be an illusion—a veil to be withdrawn in some higher state of being. But be it what it may, it supplies all the evidence upon which we can rely. If evil predominates here, we have no reason to suppose that good predominates elsewhere. All the ingenuity of theologians can never shake our conviction that facts are what we feel them to be, nor invert the plain inference from facts; and facts are just as open to one school of thought as to another.

What, then, is the net result? One insoluble doubt has haunted men's minds since thought began in the world. No answer has ever been suggested. One school of philosophers hands it to the next. It is denied in one form only to reappear in another. The question is not which system excludes the doubt, but how it expresses the doubt. Admit or deny the competence of reason in theory, we all agree that it fails in practice.

Theologians revile reason as much as Agnostics; they then appeal to it, and it decides against them. They amend their plea by excluding certain questions from its jurisdiction, and those questions include the whole difficulty. They go to revelation, and revelation replies by calling doubt, mystery. They declare that their consciousness declares just what they want it to declare. Ours declares something else. Who is to decide? The only appeal is to experience, and to appeal to experience is to admit the fundamental dogma of Agnosticism.

Is it not, then, the very height of audacity, in face of a difficulty which meets us at every turn, which has perplexed all the ablest thinkers in proportion to their ability, which vanishes in one shape only to show itself in another, to declare roundly, not only that the difficulty can be solved, but that it does not exist? Why, when no honest man will deny in private that every ultimate problem is wrapped in the profoundest mystery, do honest men proclaim in pulpits that unhesitating certainty is the duty of the most foolish and ignorant? Is it not a spectacle to make the angels laugh? We are a company of ignorant beings, feeling our way through mists and darkness, learning only by incessantly repeated blunders, obtaining a glimmering of truth by falling into every conceivable error, dimly discerning light enough for our daily needs, but hopelessly differing whenever we attempt to describe the ultimate origin or end of our paths; and yet, when one of us ventures to declare that we don't know the map of the universe as well as the map of our infinitesimal parish, he is hooted, reviled, and perhaps told that he will be damned to all eternity for his faithlessness. . . .

Gentlemen, we can only reply, wait till you have some show of agreement amongst yourselves. Wait till you can give some answer, not palpably a verbal answer, to some one of the doubts which oppress us as they oppress you. Wait till you can point to some single truth, however trifling, which has been discovered by your method, and will stand the test of discussion and verification. Wait till you can appeal to reason without in the same breath vilifying reason. Wait till your Divine revelations have something more to reveal than the hope that the hideous doubts which they suggest may possibly be without foundation.

Till then we shall be content to admit openly, what you whisper under your breath or hide in technical jargon, that the ancient secret is a secret still; that man knows nothing of the Infinite and Absolute; and that, knowing nothing, he had better not be dogmatic about his ignorance. And, meanwhile, we will endeavour to be as charitable as possible, and whilst you trumpet forth officially your contempt for our skepticism, we will at least try to believe that you are imposed upon by your own bluster.

Mark Twain

Mark Twain (Samuel Langhorne Clemens, 1835-1910) was not only America's leading humorist; he was also an important critic of America's organized religion. He mixed his puckish humor with acid reflections on conventional morals so skillfully that men did not realize how heretical he was until long after his death.

Now he has been revealed in posthumous works as a cynically bitter enemy of orthodoxy. During his lifetime he was partially suppressed by family and economic pressures. Then, fifty-two years after his death, in 1962, Harper and Row published his *Letters From the Earth*, which contained many of the anti-religious writings that had been suppressed.

About the Bible he said: "It is full of interest. It has noble poetry in it; and some clever fables; and some blood-drenched history; and some good morals, and a wealth of obscenity, and upwards of a thousand lies." About missionaries he said: "Missionarying—that least excusable of all human trades. . . . " When a Brooklyn librarian protested to him about the character of Huckleberry Finn, he replied that Huck's character was better than that of Solomon and David, and he added: "I cherish an unappeasable bitterness against the unfaithful guardians of my young life who not only permitted but compelled me to read an unexpurgated Bible through before I was fifteen years old."

It is fair to rate Mark Twain as a humanist without a formal label. The reader who devours *The Mysterious Stranger* finds an author who wants to abandon all religious illusions and rely entirely on human moral endeavor. When he wrote his philosophical essay *What Is Man?*, it seemed so irreverent to his daughter Jean that she refused to type it.

That daughter Jean figures in the first quotation from Mark Twain I have decided to include, "The War Prayer." Twain dictated it about five years before his death, but Jean strongly protested against it as sacrilegious. He accepted her veto for the time being and did not publish the prayer while Jean was alive. It was finally brought out in 1923 by Harper's, in an old edition of *Europe and Elsewhere*. Then it was seized

168

by pacifists before World War II and given wide circulation. (I was one of them.)

My second selection from Twain, "The Story of the Bad Little Boy," is typical of his early, sardonic humor, very plain and very obvious. It was published by E. Haldeman-Julius as part of the Little Blue Book, No. 668.

—P.B.

The War Prayer

(It was a time of great and exalting excitement. The country was up in arms, the war was on. . . . [I]n the churches the pastors preached devotion to flag and country, and invoked the God of Battles. . . . Sunday morning came—next day the battalions would leave for the front. . . . Then came the long prayer. . . . The burden of its supplication was that an ever-merciful and benignant Father of us all would watch over our noble young soldiers, and comfort and encourage them in their patriotic work. . . .

An aged stranger entered and moved with slow and noiseless step up the main aisle. . . . [H]e ascended to the preacher's side and stood there, waiting. . . . Listen!)

O Lord our Father, our young patriots, idols of our hearts, go forth to battle—be Thou near them! With them—in spirit—we also go forth from the sweet peace of our beloved firesides to smite the foe.

O Lord our God, help us to tear their soldiers to bloody shreds with our shells; help us to cover their smiling fields with the pale forms of their patriot dead; help us to drown the thunder of the guns with the shrieks of their wounded, writhing in pain; help us to lay waste their humble homes with a hurricane of fire; help us to wring the hearts of their unoffending widows with unavailing grief; help us to turn them out roofless with their little children to wander unfriended the wastes of their desolated land in rags and hunger and thirst, sports of the sun flames of summer and the icy winds of winter, broken in spirit, worn with travail, imploring Thee for the refuge of the grave and denied it—for our sakes who adore Thee, Lord, blast their hopes, blight their lives, protract their bitter pilgrimage, make heavy their steps, water their way with their tears, stain the white snow with the blood of their wounded feet!

We ask it in the spirit of love, of Him Who is the Source of Love, and Who is the ever-faithful refuge and friend of all that are sore beset and seek His aid with humble and contrite hearts. Amen.

(It was believed afterward that the man was a lunatic, because there was no sense in what he said.)

The Story of
a Bad Little Boy

Once there was a bad little boy whose name was Jim— though, if you will notice, you will find that bad little boys are nearly always called James in your Sunday school books. It was strange, but still it was true that this one was called Jim.

He didn't have any sick mother either—a sick mother who was pious and had the consumption, and would be glad to lie down in the grave and be at rest but for the strong love she bore her boy, and the anxiety she felt that the world might be harsh and cold toward him when she was gone.

Most bad boys in the Sunday books are named James, and have sick mothers who teach them to say "Now I lay me down," etc. and sing them to sleep with sweet plaintive voices, and then kiss them good night and kneel down by the bedside and weep. But it was different with this fellow. He was named Jim, and there wasn't anything the matter with his mother, no consumption, nor anything of that kind. She was rather stout than otherwise, and she was not pious, moreover, she was not anxious on Jim's account. She said if he were to break his neck it wouldn't be much loss. She always spanked Jim to sleep, and she never kissed him good night; on the contrary, she boxed his ears when she was ready to leave him.

Once this little bad boy stole the key of the pantry, and slipped in there and helped himself to some jam, and filled up the vessel with tar, so that his mother would never know the difference; but all at once a terrible feeling didn't come over him, and something didn't seem to whisper to him, "Is it right to disobey my mother? Isn't it sinful to do this? Where do bad little boys go who gobble up their good kind mother's jam?" And then he didn't kneel down all alone and promise never to be wicked any more, and rise up with a light, happy heart, and go and tell his mother all about it, and beg her forgiveness, and be blessed by her with tears of pride and thankfulness in her eyes.

No; that is the way with all other bad boys in the books; but it happened otherwise with this Jim, strangely enough. He ate that jam, and said it was bully, in his sinful, vulgar way; and he put in the tar, and said that was bully also, and he laughed, and observed "that the old woman would get up and snort" when she found it out; and when she did find it out, he denied knowing anything about it, and she whipped him severely, and he did the crying himself.

Once he climbed up in Farmer Acorn's apple tree to steal apples, and the limb didn't break, and he didn't fall and break his arm, and get torn by the farmer's great dog, and then languish on a sick bed for weeks, and repent and become good. Oh, no; he stole as many apples as he wanted, and came down all right; and he was all ready for the dog, too, and knocked him endways with a brick when he came to tear him.

Once he stole the teacher's pen-knife, and, when he was afraid it would be found out and he would get whipped, he slipped it into George Wilson's cap—poor widow Wilson's son, the moral boy, the good little boy of the village, who always obeyed his mother, and never told an untruth, and was fond of his lessons, and infatuated with Sunday school. And when the knife dropped from the cap and poor George hung his head and blushed, as if in conscious guilt, and the grieved teacher charged the theft upon him and was just in the very act of bringing the switch down on his trembling shoulders, a white-haired improbable justice of the peace did not suddenly appear in their midst and strike an attitude and say: "Spare this noble boy— there stands the cowering culprit! I was passing the school door at recess and, unseen myself, I saw the theft committed."

And then Jim didn't get whaled, and the venerable justice didn't read the cheerful school a homily and take George by the hand and say such a boy deserves to be exalted, and then tell him to come and make his home with him, and sweep out the office, and make fires, and run errands, and chop wood, and study law, and help his wife do household labors, and have all the balance of the time to play, and get forty cents a month, and be happy.

No; it would have happened in the books, but it didn't happen that way to Jim. No meddling old clam of a justice dropped in to make trouble, and so the model boy George got thrashed, and Jim was glad of it because, you know, Jim hated moral boys. Jim said he was "down on them milksops." Such was the coarse language of this bad, neglected boy.

But the strangest thing that ever happened to Jim was the time he went boating on Sunday, and didn't get drowned, and that other time that he got caught out in a storm when he was fishing on Sunday and didn't get struck by lightning. . . . [H]e stole his father's gun and went hunting on the Sabbath, and didn't shoot three or four of his fingers off. . . .He ran off and went to sea at last, and didn't come back and find herself sad and alone in the world, his loved ones sleeping in the quiet churchyard, and the vine-embowered home of his boyhood trumbled down and gone to decay. Ah, no, he came home as drunk as a piper, and got into the stationhouse the first thing.

And he grew up and married, and raised a large family, and brained them all with an axe one night, and got wealthy by all manner of cheating and rascality; and now he is the infernalest wickedest scoundrel in his native village, and he is universally respected and belongs to the legislature.

Voltaire

Voltaire (Francois Marie Arouet, 1694-1778) has often been called the greatest writer in all human history. He was poet, playwright, historian, philosopher and political propagandist. He was also a considerable scholar in the field of religion and a powerful opponent of Christian orthodoxy. In clerically dominated France he was sufficiently rebellious to be exiled three times and imprisoned twice for expressing heretical opinions.

His own religious classification might be described as wavering. He wavered between outright atheism and deism, usually coming down on the side of safety. He ridiculed religion with savage jibes—reading Christian theology, he said, was "like going the rounds of a lunatic asylum"— and he scorned all the major dogmas of Christianity including the Trinity, the atonement, and original sin; but in his later years he repudiated atheism so vigorously that some of his atheistic disciples considered him a traitor.

My first two selections from Voltaire concern adultery and divorce. Voltaire was not a good model for family life, and he made no attempt to conceal his scorn for conventional sexual moral codes. His personal liberties included incest, and he once declared that "marriage is the only adventure open to the cowardly." In his *Philosophical Dictionary* he published the two first selections below, mocking both marriage and sexual selfishness. It is a pity that Pope Paul VI did not read and take to heart Voltaire's gospel on adultery and divorce before he attempted, in 1974, to prevent all divorce in Italy.

My third quotation from Voltaire is also taken from his *Philosophical Dictionary*, this time as used by Geoffrey Brereton in his useful source book, *French Thought in the 18th Century,* published by David McKay. Voltaire's thoughts on tolerance will be appreciated more if it is remembered that they were spoken in a nation where the murder of Protestants was accepted as a patroitic duty. It is estimated that four hundred thousand non-Catholics left France after the Edict of Nantes, a mildly tolerant measure, was revoked in 1685. (My own Blanshard ancestors were among them.) Voltaire had become famous in the 1760s for fighting to redeem the reputation of a Protestant father who had been broken on the wheel under a false charge that he had murdered his own son. (This was the case of Jean Calais.)

Perhaps the best way to remember Voltaire is to recall a statement he once made about himself: "When I am attacked, I defend myself like a devil; but I am a good devil and end by laughing."

—P.B.

A Man Looks at Adultery and Divorce

A senior magistrate of a French town had the misfortune to have a wife who was debauched by a priest before her marriage, and who since covered herself with disgrace by public scandals: he was so moderate as to leave her without noise. This man, about forty years old, vigorous and of agreeable appearance, needs a woman; he is too scrupulous to seek to seduce another man's wife, he fears intercourse with a public woman or with a widow who would serve him as concubine. In this disquieting and sad state, he addresses to his Church a plea of which the following is a précis:

My wife is criminal, and it is I who am punished. Another woman is necessary as a comfort to my life, to my virtue even; and the sect of which I am a member refuses her to me; it forbids me to marry an honest girl. The civil laws of to-day, unfortunately founded on canon law, deprive me of the rights of humanity. The Church reduces me to seeking either the pleasures it reproves, or the shameful compensations it condemns; it tries to force me to be criminal.

I cast my eyes over all the peoples of the earth; there is not a single one except the Roman Catholic people among whom divorce and a new marriage are not natural rights.

What upheaval of the rule has therefore made among the Catholics a virtue of undergoing adultery, and a duty of lacking a wife when one has been infamously outraged by one's own?

Why is a bond that has rotted indissoluble in spite of the great law adopted by the code, *quidquid ligatur dissolubile est?* I am allowed a separation *a mensa et thoro,* and I am not allowed divorce. The law can deprive me of my wife, and it leaves me a name called "sacrament"! What a contradiction! what slavery! and under what laws did we receive birth!

What is still more strange is that this law of my Church is directly contrary to the words which this Church itself believes to have been uttered by Jesus Christ: "Whosoever shall put away his wife, except it be for fornication, and shall marry another, committeth adultery" (Matt. 19:9).

I do not examine whether the pontiffs of Rome are in the right to violate at their pleasure the law of him they regard as their master; whether when a state has need of an heir, it is permissible to repudiate her who can give it one. I do not inquire if a turbulent woman, demented, homicidal, a poisoner, should not be repudiated equally with an adulteress: I limit myself to the sad state which concerns me: God permits me to remarry, and the Bishop of Rome does not permit me.

Divorce was a practice among Catholics under all the emperors; it was also in all the dismembered states of the Roman Empire. The kings of France, those called "of the first line," almost all repudiated their wives in order to take new ones. At last came Gregory IX, enemy of the emperors and kings, who by a decree made marriage an unshakeable yoke; his decretal became the law of Europe. When the kings wanted to repudiate a wife who was an adulteress according to Jesus Christ's law, they could not succeed; it was necessary to find ridiculous pretexts. Louis the younger was obligated, to accomplish his unfortunate divorce from Eleanor of Guienne, to allege a relationship which did not exist. Henry IV, to repudiate Marguerite de Valois, pretexted a still more false cause, a refusal of consent. One had to lie to obtain a divorce legitimately.

What! a king can abdicate his crown, and without the Pope's

permission he cannot abdicate his wife! Is it possible that otherwise enlightened men have wallowed so long in this absurd ser-
vitude!

That our priests, that our monks renounce wives, to that I
consent; it is an outrage against population, it is a misfortune for
them, but they merit this misfortune which they have made for
themselves. They have been the victims of the popes who wanted
to have in them slaves, soldiers without families and without
fatherland, living solely for the Church: but I, magistrate, who
serve the state all day, I need a wife in the evening; and the
Church has not the right to deprive me of a benefit which God
accords me. The apostles were married, Joseph was married, and
I want to be. If I, Alsacian, am dependent on a priest who dwells
at Rome, if this priest has the barbarous power to rob me of a
wife, let him make a eunuch of me for the singing of *Misereres* in
his chapel.

A Woman Looks at Adultery and Divorce

Equity demands that, having recorded this note in favour of
husbands, we should also put before the public the case in favour
of wives, presented to the junta of Portugal by a Countess of
Arcira. This is the susbtance of it:

The Gospel has forbidden adultery for my husband just as
for me; he will be damned as I shall, nothing is better established.
When he committed twenty infidelities, when he gave my neck-
lace to one of my rivals, and my earrings to another, I did not ask
the judges to have him shaved, to shut him up among monks and
to give me his property. And I, for having imitated him once, for
having done with the most handsome young man in Lisbon what
he did every day with impunity with the most idiotic strumpets of

the court and the town, have to answer at the bar before licentiates each of whom would be at my feet if we were alone together in my closet; have to endure at the court the usher cutting off my hair which is the most beautiful in the world; and being shut up among nuns who have no common sense, deprived of my dowry and my marriage covenants, with all my property given to my coxcomb of a husband to help him seduce other women and to commit fresh adulteries.

I ask if it is just, and if it is not evident that the laws were made by cuckolds?

In answer to my plea I am told that I should be happy not to be stoned at the city gate by the canons, the priests of the parish and the whole populace. This was the practice among the first nation of the earth, the chosen nation, the cherished nation, the only one which was right when all the others were wrong.

To these barbarities I reply that when the poor adulteress was presented by her accusers to the Master of the old and new law, He did not have her stoned; that on the contrary He reproached them with their injustice, that he laughed at them by writing on the ground with his finger, that he quoted the old Hebraic proverb—"He that is without sin among you, let him first cast a stone at her"; that then they all retired, the oldest fleeing first, because the older they were the most adulteries had they committed.

The doctors of canon law answer me that this history of the adulteress is related only in the Gospel of St. John, that it was not inserted there until later. Leonitus, Maldonat, affirm that it is not to be found in a single ancient Greek copy; that none of the twenty-three early commentators mentions it. Origen, St. Jerome, St. John Chrysostom, Theophilact, Nonnus, do not recognize it at all. It is not to be found in the Syriac Bible, it is not in Ulphilas' version.

That is what my husband's advocates say, they who would have me not only shaved, but also stoned.

But the advocates who pleaded for me say that Ammonius, author of the third century, recognized this story as true, and that if St. Jerome rejects it in some places, he adopts it in others; that, in a word, it is authentic today. I leave there, and I say to my husband: "If you are without sin, shave me, imprison me, take my property; but if you have committed more sins than I have, it is for me to shave you, to have you imprisoned, and to seize your fortune. In justice these things should be equal."

My husband answers that he is my superior and my chief, that he is more than an inch taller, that he is shaggy as a bear; that consequently I owe him everything, and that he owes me nothing.

But I ask if Queen Anne of England is not her husband's chief? if her husband the Prince of Denmark, who is her High Admiral, does not owe her entire obedience? and if she would not have him condemned by the court of peers if the little man's infidelity were in question? It is therefore clear that if the women do not have the men punished, it is when they are not the stronger.

Tolerance

What is tolerance?—it is the consequence of humanity. We are all formed of frailty and error; let us pardon reciprocally each other's folly—that is the first law of nature.

It is clear that the individual who persecutes a man, his brother, because he is not of the same opinion, is a monster. That admits of no difficulty. But the government! but the magistrates! but the princes! how do they treat those who have another worship than theirs?

Madmen, who have never been able to give worship to the God who made you! Miscreants, whom the example of the Noachides, the learned Chinese, the Parsees and all the sages, has never been able to lead! Monsters, who need superstitions as crows' gizzards need carrion! you have been told it already, and there is nothing else to tell you—if you have two religions in your countries, they will cut each other's throat; if you have thirty religions, they will dwell in peace. Look at the great Turk, he governs Guebres, Banians, Greek Christians, Nestorians, Romans. The first who tried to stir up tumult would be impaled; and everyone is tranquil.

Of all religions, the Christian is without doubt the one which should inspire tolerance most, although up to now the Christians have been the most intolerant of all men. The Christian Church was divided in its cradle, and was divided even in the persecutions which, under the first emperors, it sometimes endured. Often the martyr was regarded as an apostate by his brethen, and the Carpocratian Christian expired beneath the sword of the Roman executioner, excommunicated by the Ebionite Christian, that which Ebionite was anathema to the Sabellian.

This horrible discord, which has lasted for so many centuries is a very striking lesson that we should pardon each other's errors; discord is the great ill of mankind; and tolerance is the only remedy for it.

There is nobody who is not in agreement with this truth, whether he meditates soberly in his study, or peaceably examines the truth with his friends. Why then do the same men who admit in private indulgence, kindness, justice, rise in public with so much fury against these virtues?

I possess a dignity and a power founded on ignorance and credulity; I walk on the heads of the men who lie prostrate at my feet; if they should rise and look me in the face, I am lost; I must bind them to the ground, therefore, with iron chains.

Thus have reasoned the men whom centuries of bigotry have made powerful. They have other powerful men beneath them, and these have still others, who all enrich themselves with the spoils of the poor, grow fat on their blood, and laugh at their stupidity. They all detest tolerance, as partisans, grown rich at the public expense, fear to render their accounts and as tyrants dread the word *liberty*. And then, to crown everything, they hire fanatics to cry at the top of their voices: "Respect my master's absurdities, tremble, pay and keep your mouths shut."

It is thus that a great part of the world was long treated; but to-day, when so many sects make a balance of power, what course to take with them? Every sect, as one knows, is a ground of error; there are no sects of geometers, algebraists, arithmeticians, because all the propositions of geometry, algebra and arithmetic are true. In every other science one may be deceived.

If it were permitted to reason consistently in religious matters, it is clear that we all ought to become Jews, because Jesus Christ our Saviour was born a Jew, lived a Jew, died a Jew, and that he said expressly that He was accomplishing, that He was fulfilling the Jewish religion. But it is clearer still that we ought to be tolerant of one another, because we are all weak, inconsistent, liable to fickleness and error. Shall a reed laid low in the mud by the wind say to a fellow reed fallen in the opposite direction: "Crawl as I crawl, wretch, or I shall petition that you be torn up by the roots and burned"?

Joseph Wheless

Probably the most bitter and direct attacks on Christianity ever made by an American writer were not made by Tom Paine, Robert Ingersoll, or Clarence Darrow but by a relatively unknown military man named Joseph Wheless. Wheless's two important books were *Is It God's Word?*, a general attack on the Bible, and *Forgery in Christianity*, an even more bitter attack on certain church deceptions, published in 1930 by Alfred A. Knopf.

The first of these books was published in 1920 by the author. Although the first book was praised to the skies by H. L. Mencken, and Wheless gained a considerable vogue for several years among *American Mercury* readers, he never achieved broad recognition. Even Mencken finally described him as "truculent in tone," and he was all of that. Wheless's description of the Old Testament God in *Is It God's Word?* is more or less typical of his style: "He reeks with the blood of murders unnumbered, and is personally a murderer and assassin, by stealth and treachery; a pitiless monster of bloody vengeance; a relentless and terrifying bully and terrorist; a synonym for partiality and injustice; a vain braggart; a false prophet; an arrant and shameless liar." At times Wheless engaged in brilliant satire.

Wheless was a man of considerable scholarship who had served for many years as a legal officer in the headquarters of the judge advocate of the United States Army. One reason for his inability to secure "respectable" publishers for all his books was that he chose to single out the most sensitive areas of religious belief for his assaults. I have chosen two of those areas to illustrate his combative power, the genealogy of Jesus in the New Testament and the virginity of Mary. Both selections are taken from his work, *Is It God's Word?*

—P.B.

Geneologies of Jesus

Luke names and specifies forty-three generations from David to Jesus, instead of Matthew's twenty-eight; and only three names of the two contradictory lists are the same, except David at one end and Jesus at the other, and the immediate ancestry at both ends is totally different. For comparison, here are the Sacred Genealogies as vouched for by two inspired biographers:

MATTHEW (i, 6-16)	LUKE (iii, 23-31)
1. David	1. David
2. Solomon	2. Nathan
3. Roboam	3. Mattatha
4. Abia	4. Menan
5. Asa	5. Melea
6. Josaphat	6. Eliakim
7. Joram	7. Jonan
8. Ozias	8. Joseph
9. Joatham	9. Juda
10. Achaz	10. Simeon
11. Ezekias	11. Levi
12. Manasses	12. Matthat
13. Amon	13. Jorim
14. Josias	14. Eliezer
15. Jechonias	15. Jose
16. Salathiel	16. Er
17. Zorobabel	17. Elmodam
18. Abiud	18. Cosam
19. Eliakim	19. Addi

20. Azor	20. Melchi
21. Sadoe	21. Neri
22. Achim	22. Salathiel
23. Eliud	23. Zorobabel
24. Eleazar	24. Rhesa
25. Matthan	25. Joanna
26. Jacob	26. Juda
27. Joseph	27. Joseph
28. Jesus	28. Semei
	29. Mattathias
	30. Maath
	31. Nagge
	32. Esli
	33. Naum
	34. Amos
	35. Mattathias
	36. Joseph
	37. Janna
	38. Melchi
	39. Levi
	40. Matthat
	41. Heli
	42. Joseph
	43. Jesus

The Virgin Birth

We will briefly inspect the miraculous pregnancy of the Ever-Virgin Mother (who had more than half a dozen children), and the circumstances of her first-born Joshua or Jesus.

Matthew again is our inspired Historian. He relates that,

"When as his Mother Mary was espoused to Joseph, before they came together, she was found with child from the Holy Ghost" (i, 18); that Joseph felt quite naturally disposed to "put her away privily"; but that he dreamed that an Angel of Yahweh told him to fear not to accept his wife Mary, "for that which is conceived in her is of the Holy Ghost" (v, 20). This dream seems to have quite satisfied Joseph, though he had never heard of any Holy Ghost, and no such person of the Christian Trinity is recorded in the Hebrew Scriptures. So Joseph, "being raised from sleep," did as —he dreamed that—the angel of Yahweh had bidden him, and took unto himself his wife: "And knew her not till she had brought forth her first-born son" (vv. 24-25).

Thus we learn, from Matthew, that the news of this pregnancy of his wife by the Holy Ghost was first broken to Joseph in a dream or he dreamed that the Holy Ghost was the author of it. When, Inspiration vouchsafes not directly; but it is readily deducted that it was not till at least three months after the secret Visitation by the Holy Ghost took place. . . . Also, that it was several months after is indicated by the fact that Joseph then took her unto himself, "and knew her not *till* she had brought forth her first-born son"—thus evidently a considerable space of time, as the fact of Joseph's marital self-restraint is specially noted by inspiration.

This, too (parenthetically), disproves the Dogma that Mary remained immaculate and Ever-Virgin; for, that Joseph knew her not "till" she had given birth to her *first born* son, argues that he *did* "know her" carnally thereafter; and her "*first born*" son argues others born thereafter. So a very favorite Fallacy of the Fathers Celibate is exploded; to say nothing of the virginity destroying effects of the births of a half a dozen brothers and sisters of Jesus: "his brothers, James and Joses, and Simon, and Judas, and his sisters" (Matt. xiii, 55, 56; Mark vi, 2-3); and Paul tells us of seeing His Apostle friend "James, the Lord's brother" (Gal. i, 19).

But here again Luke as usual contradicts Matthew's story of Joseph's dream revelation by the Angel to himself of the origin of his wife's pregnancy. Luke goes into much detail relating that the Angel Gabriel, in the six months after his like mission to Mary's cousin Elizabeth, was sent from Yahweh to Nazareth, "to a virgin espoused to a man whose name was Joseph, and the virgin's name was Mary" (Luke ii, 26-27). . . . Mary remained with Elizabeth for three months until John Baptist was born to Elizabeth.

It may, in a word, be wondered how any sort of "divinity" or odor of sanctity could be attached by intelligent and modern people to this John, surnamed the Baptist. He was a wild, uncouth dirty Desert Dervish, dwelling in the Judean wilderness, of the Nazareth type, with never a haircut or shave in his life; he wore old bran sacks strapped to his waist for his scanty clothes, and for regular diet ate desert grasshoppers, evidently raw (Matt. iii, 4). He spent his life and his voice idly in the wilderness crying "prepare the way for Yahweh"—and not for Yahweh's Son and his own cousin Jesus. That his cousin Joshua-Jesus was any different from the family type does not appear. . . .

We may here note, for what it is worth in support of the orthodox Faith, that there was no novelty at all in Virgin Births from Gods in the ancient religions. It was a commonplace happening enough, which any superstitiously inclined Pagan or Hebrew would readily accept in fullness of faith. . . . The Great God of the Greeks, Zeus, Heaven Father, was also the prolific author of virgin births; of which we cite only the well known and highly accredited instances of his Swan-form copulation with Leda, the miraculous product of which were the holy twins Castor and Pollux; and his intrigue with Io, which resulted in the son Epaphus. The Roman God Mars likewise kept amorous tryst with the Vestal Virgin Rhea Silvia, of which the celebrated twins Romulus and Remus resulted. . . .

Virgin births by Gods are thus seen to have been either very frequent actualities in the good old Hebrew-Pagan times, or priestly assurance and popular credulity passed them as miraculous events worthy of the most holy faith and credence.

Andrew D. White

One of the most famous works on religion produced by an American writer during the nineteenth century was Andrew D. White's two-volume classic *A History of the Warfare of Science with Theology in Christendom*. Heretics could not have secured a more respectable ally than White. A diplomat of high standing and the first president of Cornell, White's bourgeois pedigree was as impeccable as his beard and his Prince Albert. Nominally he was a Christian, a sentimental liberal Protestant who sought to cleanse his own church of superstition without destroying it.

He insisted that science was not opposed to religion, as such, but to dogmatic and ignorant theology. In the introduction to his 1896 work he said, "I simply try to aid in letting the light of historical truth into that decaying mass of outworn thought which attaches the modern world to medieval conceptions of Christianity, and which still lingers among us—a most serious barrier to religion and morals, and a menace to the whole normal evolution of society."

When he became president of Cornell, he was made the target of a bitter orthodox campaign that pictured him as the head of an institution "preaching Darwinism and atheism." Finally, he struck back at the whole orthodox establishment of his time, indicting the theologians in the name of modern science.

White's most effective shots were directed at self-righteous conservative Protestantism. His criticisms seem somewhat overdone in the light of liberal-Protestant growth in recent years, but at the time of their publication they were badly needed to balance the narrow and self-righteous anti-Catholicism of the period. "The Lutheran Church," he declared, "resulting from the great religious revolution of the sixteenth century, became immediately after the death of Luther, and remained during generations, more inexcusably cruel and intolerant than Catholicism had ever been; the revolution which enthroned Calvinism in large parts of the British Empire and elsewhere brought new forms of unreason, oppression and unhappiness." After attacking the popes and the Inquisition for their stupidities and cruelties in handling Copernicus and Galileo, White "balanced" his judgment by the following anti-Protestant criticism in which he actually used some words of praise for Pope Leo XIII. This excerpt is taken from Volume One of the original edition of White's *History*. The second excerpt is from Volume Two.

—P.B.

Protestant Foes of Light

Nothing is more unjust than to cast especial blame for all this resistance to science upon the Roman Church. The Protestant Church, though rarely able to be so severe, has been more blameworthy.

The persecution of Galileo and his compeers by the older Church was mainly at the beginning of the seventeenth century; the persecution of Robertson, Smith and Winchell, and Woodrow and Toy, and the young professors at Beyrout by various Protestant authorities was near the end of the nineteenth century. These earlier persecutions by Catholicism were strictly in accordance with principles held at that time by all religionists, Catholic and Protestant, throughout the world. These later persecutions by Protestants were in defiance of principles which all Protestants today hold or pretend to hold, and none made louder claim to hold them than the very sects which persecuted these eminent Christian men of our day, men whose crime was that they were intelligent enough to accept the science of their time, and honest enough to acknowledge it.

Most unjustly, then, would Protestantism taunt Catholicism for excluding knowledge of astronomical truths from European Catholic universities in the seventeenth and eighteenth centuries, while real knowledge of geological and biological and anthropological truth is denied or pitifully diluted in so many American Protestant colleges and universities in the nineteenth century.

Nor has Protestantism the right to point with scorn to the Catholic *Index*, and to lay stress on the fact that nearly every really important book in the last three centuries has been forbidden by it, so long as young men in so many American Protestant universities and colleges are nursed with "ecclesiastical pap" rather than with real thought, and directed to the works of "solemnly constituted imposters," or to sundry "approved courses of reading" while they are studiously kept aloof from such leaders of modern thought as Darwin, Spencer, Huxley, Draper, and Lecky.

It may indeed be justly claimed by Protestantism that some of the former strongholds of her bigotry have been liberated; but, on the other hand, Catholicism can point to the fact that Pope Leo XIII, now happily reigning, has made a noble change as regards open dealing with documents. . . . The Vatican Library, with its masses of historical materials, has been thrown open to Protestant and Catholic scholars alike, and this privilege has been freely used by men representing all shades of religious thought.

As to the older errors, the whole civilized world was at fault, Protestant as well as Catholic. It was not the fault of religion; it was the fault of that short-sighted linking of theological dogmas to scriptural texts which, in utter defiance of the words and works of the Blessed Founder of Christianity, narrow-minded, loud-voiced men are ever prone to substitute for religion. Justly it is said by one of the most eminent among contemporary Anglican divines that "it is because they have mistaken the dawn for a conflagration that theologians have so often been foes of light."

Theology and Epidemics

A very striking feature in recorded history has been the re-currence of great pestilences. . . . In the Middle Ages they raged from time to time throughout Europe: such plagues as the Black Death and the sweating sickness swept vast multitudes, the best authorities estimating that of the former, at the middle of the fourteenth century, more than half the population of England died, and that twenty-five millions of people perished in various parts of Europe. . . .

From the earliest records we find such pestilences attributed to the wrath or malice of unseen powers. This had been the pre-vailing view even in the most cultured ages before the establish-ment of Christianity. . . . in Judea, the scriptural records of various plagues set upon the earth by the Divine fiat as a punish-ment for sin show the continuance of this mode of thought. . . . During nearly twenty centuries since the rise of Christianity, and down to a period within living memory, at the appearance of any pestilence the Christian authorities, instead of devising sanitary measures, have very generally preached the necessity of immedi-ate atonement for offenses against the Almighty. . . .

The main cause of this immense sacrifice of life is now known to have been the want of hygienic precaution. . . . And here certain theological reasonings came in to resist the proper evolution of a proper sanitary theory. Out of the Orient had been poured into the thinking of Western Europe the theological idea that the abasement of man adds to the glory of God; that indig-nity to the body may secure salvation to the soul; hence, that cleanliness betokens pride and filthiness humility.

Living in filth was regarded by great numbers of holy men,

who set an example to the Church and to society, as an evidence of sanctity. St. Jerome and the Breviary of the Roman Church dwell with unction on the fact that St. Hilarion lived his whole life long in utter physical uncleanliness; St. Athanasius glorifies St. Anthony because he had never washed his feet; St. Abraham's most striking evidence of holiness was that for fifty years he washed neither his hands nor his feet; St. Sylvia never washed any part of her body save her fingers; St. Euphrasia belonged to a convent in which the nuns religiously abstained from bathing; St. Mary of Egypt was eminent for filthiness; St. Simon Stylites was in this respect unspeakable—the least that can be said is that he lived in ordure and stench intolerable to his visitors. The *Lives of the Saints* dwell with complacency on the statement that, when sundry Eastern monks showed a disposition to wash themselves the Almighty manifested his displeasure by drying up a neighboring stream until the bath which it had supplied was destroyed. . . .

In the principal towns of Europe, as well as in the country at large, down to a recent period, the most ordinary sanitary precautions were neglected, and pestilences continued to be attributed to the wrath of God or the malice of Satan. As to the wrath of God, a new and powerful impulse was given to this belief in the Church toward the end of the sixth century by St. Gregory the Great. . . .

The whole evolution of modern history, not only ecclesiastical but civil, has been largely affected by the wealth transferred to the clergy at such periods. It was noted that in the fourteenth century, after the great plague, the Black Death, had passed, an immensely increased proportion of the landed and personal property of every European country was in the hands of the Church. Well did a great ecclesiastic remark that "pestilences are the harvests of the ministers of God."

PAPERBACKS AVAILABLE FROM PROMETHEUS BOOKS

SCIENCE AND THE PARANORMAL

_____ 12.95 Ancient Astronauts, Cosmic Collisions   *William Stiebing, Jr.*
_____ 11.95 The Bermuda Triangle Mystery—Solved   *Larry Kusche*
_____ 13.95 ESP and Parapsychology   *C. E. M. Hansel*
_____ 11.95 Flim-Flam!   *James Randi*
_____ 12.95 The Fringe of the Unknown   *L. Sprague de Camp*
_____ 12.95 The Gemini Syndrome   *Culver and Ianna*
_____ 11.95 The Loch Ness Mystery Solved   *Ronald Binns*
_____ 16.95 Paranormal Borderlands of Science   *edited by Kendrick Frazier*
_____ 13.95 Psychic Paradoxes   *John Booth*
_____ 13.95 The Psychology of the Psychic   *Marks and Kammann*
_____ 15.95 Science Confronts the Paranormal   *edited by Kendrick Frazier*
_____ 16.95 A Skeptic's Handbook of Parapsychology   *edited by Paul Kurtz*
_____ 13.95 The Spiritualists   *Ruth Brandon*
_____ 10.95 The Truth About Uri Geller   *James Randi*
_____ 11.95 UFOs: The Public Deceived   *Philip J. Klass*
_____ 13.95 The UFO Verdict   *Robert Sheaffer*

PHILOSOPHY

_____ 11.95 Animal Rights and Human Morality   *Bernard Rollin*
_____ 10.95 The Art of Deception   *Nicholas Capaldi*
_____ 17.95 Business Ethics   *edited by Snoeyenbos, Almeder, and Humber*
_____ 17.95 Contemporary Analytic and Linguistic Philosophies   *edited by E. D. Klemke*
_____ 17.95 Contemporary Readings in Social and Political Ethics   *edited by Brodsky, Troyer, and Vance*
_____ 16.95 Decisions in Philosophy of Religion   *William B. Williamson*
_____ 13.95 Esthetics Contemporary   *edited by Richard Kostelanetz*
_____ 16.95 Ethics and the Legal Profession   *edited by Davis and Elliston*
_____ 17.95 Ethics and the Search for Values   *edited by Navia and Kelly*
_____ 9.95 Ethics Without God   *Kai Nielsen*
_____ 10.95 Exuberance   *Paul Kurtz*
_____ 11.95 Good and Evil   *Richard Taylor*
_____ 14.95 An Invitation to Philosophy   *edited by Capaldi, Kelly, and Navia*
_____ 17.95 Journeys Through Philosophy (Revised)   *edited by Capaldi, Navia, and Kelly*
_____ 15.95 Latin American Philosophy in the Twentieth Century   *edited by Jorge J. E. Gracia*
_____ 3.95 On Liberty   *John Stuart Mill*
_____ 10.95 Philosophy: An Introduction   *Antony Flew*
_____ 15.95 Philosophy and Science Fiction   *edited by Michael Philips*
_____ 16.95 Philosophy and Sex (Revised)   *edited by Baker and Elliston*
_____ 4.95 The Politics   *Aristotle*
_____ 4.95 The Prince   *Niccolo Machiavelli*
_____ 11.95 The Problem of God   *Peter A. Angeles*
_____ 5.95 The Republic   *Plato*
_____ 3.95 The Second Treatise on Civil Government   *John Locke*
_____ 3.95 The Subjection of Women   *John Stuart Mill*
_____ 9.95 Thinking Straight   *Antony Flew*
_____ 11.95 The Worlds of the Early Greek Philosophers   *edited by Wilbur and Allen*
_____ 11.95 The Worlds of Hume and Kant   *edited by Wilbur and Allen*
_____ 11.95 The Worlds of Plato and Aristotle   *edited by Wilbur and Allen*

POPULAR SCIENCE

_____ 12.95 In the Beginning   *Chris McGowan*
_____ 12.95 The Magic Numbers of Dr. Matrix   *Martin Gardner*
_____ 11.95 The Roving Mind   *Isaac Asimov*

SOCIAL SCIENCES AND CURRENT EVENTS

HEALTH ISSUES

NEW CONCEPTS IN HUMAN SEXUALITY

LITERATURE, CRITICISM AND BIOGRAPHY

FRONTIERS IN EDUCATION

THE SKEPTIC'S BOOKSHELF

____ 10.95 The Age of Reason *Thomas Paine*
____ 15.95 An Anthology of Atheism and Rationalism *edited by Gordon Stein*
____ 10.95 Atheism: The Case Against God *George H. Smith*
____ 8.95 The Atheist Debater's Handbook *B. C. Johnson*
____ 12.95 Bertrand Russell on God and Religion *edited by Al Seckel*
____ 13.95 Judaism Beyond God: A Radical New Way to Be Jewish *Sherwin T. Wine*
____ 11.95 The Mystery of the Kingdom of God *Albert Schweitzer*
____ 15.95 The Origins of Christianity *R. Joseph Hoffmann*
____ 12.95 Some Mistakes of Moses *Robert G. Ingersoll*

HUMANISM

____ 11.95 The Best of Robert Ingersoll *edited by Roger E. Greeley*
____ 7.95 The Humanist Alternative *edited by Paul Kurtz*
____ 12.95 Humanist Ethics *edited by Morris B. Storer*
____ 6.95 A Humanist Funeral Service *Corliss Lamont*
____ 2.95 Humanist Manifestos I and II
____ 3.95 A Humanist Wedding Service *Corliss Lamont*
____ 10.95 In Defense of Secular Humanism *Paul Kurtz*
____ 2.95 A Secular Humanist Declaration

The books listed above can be obtained from your book dealer or directly from Prometheus Books. Please check off the appropriate books. Remittance must accompany all orders from individuals. Please include $2.00 postage and handling for first book, .75 for each additional book (4.50 maximum). (N.Y.S. residents please add applicable sales tax.)

Send to _____
                            (Please type or print clearly)
Address _____
City _____ State _____ Zip _____
Charge my ☐ **VISA**   Amount Enclosed _____
                ☐ **MasterCard**
Acct. _____   Phone orders (outside NYS) call toll free: 800-421-0351.
Exp. Date _____ Tel. # _____   In NYS: 716-837-2475
Signature _____   Please allow 3-6 weeks for delivery

PROMETHEUS BOOKS
700 E. Amherst Street, Buffalo, NY 14215